Managing Operational Risk in Financial Markets

This book is dedicated to my father Haji Mir Mohammad Hussain.

Managing Operational Risk in Financial Markets

Amanat Hussain

BUTTERWORTH
HEINEMANN

OXFORD AUCKLAND BOSTON JOHANNESBURG MELBOURNE NEW DELHI

Butterworth-Heinemann
Linacre House, Jordan Hill, Oxford OX2 8DP
225 Wildwood Avenue, Woburn, MA 01801-2041
A division of Reed Educational and Professional Publishing Ltd

℞ A member of the Reed Elsevier plc group

First published 2000

British Library Cataloguing in Publication Data
Hussain, Amanat
   Managing operational risk in financial markets
   1. Risk management   2. Financial institutions – Investments – Management
   I. Title
   332.6

ISBN 0 7506 4732 9

Typeset by Avocet Typeset, Brill, Aylesbury, Bucks
Printed and bound in Great Britain by Biddles Ltd, www.Biddles.co.uk

PLANT A TREE

BTCV
British Trust for
Conservation Volunteers

FOR EVERY TITLE THAT WE PUBLISH, BUTTERWORTH-HEINEMANN
WILL PAY FOR BTCV TO PLANT AND CARE FOR A TREE.

Contents

Acknowledgements

It is hard to know where to start when writing the acknowledgements; this makes them the most difficult part of the book to write. However, I am indebted to all the individuals and companies that took part in the survey and provided information for this book. I would also like to thank all the individuals who contributed by providing articles and reports about derivatives operations and controls.

I owe special thanks to Bsharat Hussain for his valued contribution to the book.

1 | Introduction

The financial markets industry has undergone tremendous changes over the past few years. The main drivers for change have been, and continue to be, globalization, advances in information technology and telecommunication. With the current trends in mergers and acquisitions creating larger and larger institutions and the developments in technology, the pace of change within the industry is accelerating. The resulting competitive and challenging environment makes it imperative that financial institutions understand the risk that they are facing and have effective controls and procedures, systems and skills in place to deal with them.

The developments in technology provide financial institutions the ability to analyse and react to market information much more quickly. The continued development in data management and data analysis techniques and capabilities along with changes in communication technology mean that market data and rate movements are available to all institutions almost instantaneously across the globe. The ability to receive, assimilate, analyse and react to this flow of information will provide the key competitive advantage to an institution.

While market and credit remain the key focus of risk management, the importance of operational risk in this volatile, high volume, and high technology environment is also enhanced. Organizational structure and culture along with technical infrastructure and staff commitment and skills play an increasingly important role. In this environment, the presence of a strong and an effective risk management infrastructure is of paramount importance to a financial institution. This not only requires the development of robust models for monitoring market and credit risk but also new approaches for understanding and managing operational risk. The nature of operational risk is that it does not easily lend itself to quantitative measurements and analysis. Therefore, in developing risk management infrastructure, institutions need to adopt a pragmatic approach that utilizes the best available tools and technology as well as common sense.

The purpose of this book is to outline what is important in terms of risk management and to focus on operational risk as a key activity in managing risk on an enterprise-wide basis. While risk management has always been an integral part of financial activity, the 1990s has seen risk management establish itself as a key function within banks and other financial institutions. With greater emphasis on ensuring that money is not lost through adverse market conditions, counterparty failure or inappropriate controls, systems or people, risk management has become a discipline in its own right within financial markets.

The current era of risk management is synonymous with the development of the derivatives markets. Two key events in the early 1970s provided impetus for the increased use of derivatives. The first was the collapse of the Bretton Woods agreement in 1973 that led to a system of more or less freely floating exchange rates among many of the major trading countries. The subsequent requirement for the measurement and management of foreign exchange risk led to the development and increased use of derivatives products. The second key development in 1973 was the publication of the ideas underlying the Black–Scholes formula that provided the conceptual framework and basic tools for risk measurement and management.

The introduction of financial derivatives products on the Chicago Board of Trade (CBOT) and Chicago Mercantile Exchange (CME) during the 1970s and early 1980s and the introduction of currency and interest rate swaps in 1981 and 1982 paved the way for the explosion in the use of derivatives products for portfolio hedging, risk management and income generation. The 1980s and 1990s has seen a tremendous growth in exchanges trading futures and options contracts. The London International Financial Futures and Options Exchange that started trading in 1982 was followed by the Singapore International Monetary Exchange in 1984 and the Hong Kong Futures Exchange in 1985. Marche a Terme International de France (MATIF) in France opened in 1986 and Deutsche Terminborse (DTB) in Germany opened in 1990. Numerous exchanges around the world have sprung up during the 1990s.

In parallel with the development of the exchange traded derivatives, over-the-counter (OTC) derivatives products have also seen tremendous growth both in terms of their use and their characteristics. The nature of the OTC derivatives products, which allows their structure and cashflow characteristics to be tailored to match the user's risk/reward profile, makes them an indispensable tool for risk management. The development of the OTC market added an array of new products including forward rate agreements (FRAs), swaps, options, swaptions, cap and floors that can be based on financials, equities, commodities or metals.

There have been some major advances in technology and communication in the recent years. This has impacted both the organizational culture and structure and the flow of information within the organizations. The information revolution of the 1990s has forced institutions to re-evaluate their structure in order to become more flexible, productive and profitable. This is leading to flatter organizations where tiers of middle management have been removed. With better and more efficient flow of information, organizations are becoming more dispersed, decentralized and federal in nature. The move away from functional hierarchies to more project based organizations provides the flexibility that is needed but it also creates control problems that need to be addressed.

Advances in technology are allowing institutions to trade more efficiently, leading to greater volumes of transactions during periods of market volatility. With access to data through many channels, increased automation and straight through processing, there is a significant increase in data processing and management requirements. There is an increasing requirement for organizations to provide and share information with their customers and partners on a real time basis. As the information systems become more integrated, the boundaries between organizations are beginning to blur. The development of the Internet and intranets has speeded up the flow of information and is set to have a tremendous impact in the banking industry. The increased flexibility and growth in the speed and volume of information flows places greater demands on the organizational infrastructure and staff and requires more efficient and effective monitoring and control systems.

In this flexible, integrated, decentralized and federal financial institution, the requirement for an enterprise wide approach to risk management is fundamental to its successful operation. With increased globalization and greater emphasis of customer service, institutions will need to develop strategies for all the risks that they face and not just concentrate on market or credit risk. In this global and federal organization personnel, technology, legal, reputation and control risks become much more significant.

In this environment, companies need to update and upgrade the operational and structural models. They need to move away from imposing risk controls on the various functional units and develop a risk management culture within the organizations where all staff have the responsibility for risk management.

Events in the 1990s have focused attention on monitoring and control functions and the need for enterprise wide risk management. Banks and financial institutions, which were traditionally considered to be well managed and relatively low risk institutions, are now having to concentrate on building their risk management infrastructure. Managing risk is now *the* paramount topic within the financial sector. The emphasis has switched from making money to not losing it. Recurring major losses through the 1990s have shocked financial institutions into placing much grater emphasis on risk management and controls. The collapse of Barings, the losses at Metallgesellschaft, Orange County, Diawa and Sumitomo as result of a lack of procedures, systems or managerial control have demonstrated to the organizations the need to broaden the scope of their risk management activity from merely looking at market and credit risk. This has brought into focus the need for managing operational risk. Operational risk can only be managed on an enterprise wide basis as it includes the entire process of policies, culture, procedures, expertise and systems that an institution needs in order to manage all the risks resulting from its financial transactions. In fact, in order to effectively manage market and credit risks it is necessary to have the relevant skills and expertise in the staff, technical and organizational infrastructure, as well as monitoring and control systems. As all of these are components of operational risk, it then becomes apparent that an integrated risk management approach needs to focus on operational risk.

With any activity that has an element of risk associated with it, the construction of effective and meaningful controls and procedures, and their proper implementation, are prerequisite to safe operation.

Operational risk is no more or less important than trading or counterparty or credit risk. It is, however, an area that has traditionally received less attention and is frequently considered to be less importance. Events in the industry have all too graphically illustrated the danger of concentrating attention on what is considered to be the 'sharp end' of the business.

This book develops a new model for managing operational risk within the financial markets industry. As well as defining the major types of risk and assessing the importance of effective operational risk management, this book provides a detailed framework for managing operational risk taking into account the developments in technology as well as the latest techniques in organization development. It reviews the organizational development techniques available to financial institutions which can be used to 'embed' a risk management culture within these organizations. This book reviews the role for the operations area and outlines the cultural changes and the paradigm shift that is required in order redefine this area and its role in a modern knowledge based organization of the twenty-first century.

In writing this book I have addressed the following major issues:

1 Outline the major types of risks that can affect a financial institution and define the constituents of operational risk.

2 Review current organizational structures, people, processes and technology within financial institutions for the operations area.

3 Analyse the cultural changes and paradigm shifts that are necessary to redefine the operations function within a knowledge based financial institution.

4 Review some of the organizational development techniques, particularly business process reengineering, organizational learning and knowledge management, that can be adopted to help manage financial institutions in a continuously changing and increasingly competitive environment.

5 The role of technology in facilitating the paradigm shift that is necessary for institutions to gain competitive advantage as well as managing risk through operational excellence.

6 Develop a framework for an enterprise wide information system to facilitate effective risk management.

7 Outline a framework and develop a model for managing operational risk and define an updated role for the operations area within financial institutions.

2 | Financial losses over the past few years

The range and use of derivatives has grown dramatically over recent years. Whether transacted on the regulated exchanges (i.e. CBOT, CME, LIFFE, SIMEX etc.) or over-the-counter, derivatives are widely used by banks, corporates, financial institutions, fund management companies and other organizations to achieve a variety of trading or hedging objectives. Derivatives play and will continue to play an important role in the world's trading and financial systems. Yet many, both inside and outside the financial markets, remain uncomfortable with derivatives activity. The instruments are seen as inherently risky, complex and obscure. The collapse of Barings, in 1995, as a result of unsustainable trading losses and other high profile losses within the industry has further reinforced this perception. The most common assumption about the derivatives business is that it is high risk. To quote the *Financial Times*, 4 March 1995:

> A derivative is like a razor. You can use it to shave yourself and make yourself attractive to your girlfriend. You can slit her throat with it. Or you can use it to commit suicide.

Other notable quotes are 'Wild cards in international finance' by a member of the American Congress and 'the dreaded derivatives' by the Governor of the Bank of England in the aftermath of the Barings collapse.

These comments after the collapse of Britain's oldest bank were very emotive in nature. Derivative instruments perform a very important risk management and hedging function. The versatility of the derivatives instrument lies in the fact that their structure and characteristics can be customized to the user's needs. OTC derivatives can be custom-tailored with unique structures and payoff functions that effectively dovetail with a client's particular risk profile and outlook. However, the leverage nature of the product means that very large exposures can be gained with relatively small capital outlay. Unless the associated exposure and risk is monitored and controlled effectively, the potential for high financial losses is undoubtedly very real.

The past few years have seen a number of high profile risk management problems within the financial markets industry including:

- $1.06 billion provision[1] made, in 1998, to compensate for anticipated losses on Credit Suisse First Boston's (CSFB) Russian operations. CSFB had hedged their rouble exposure by buying currency forwards on the Moscow Interbank Currency Exchange (Micex). However, of the $1.06 billion provision, $637 million was the result of the losses sustained on the currency forwards. These derivative losses occurred because Micex and several Russian banks either defaulted or terminated the contracts written with CSFB as the counterparty. This was an example of losses due to country risk.

- $3.5 billion bailout of the Long-Term Capital Management fund that specialized in the highly leveraged and complex derivatives contracts.

- The collapse of Barings as a result of unsustainable trading losses on trading the futures contracts on the Singapore International Monetary Exchange (SIMEX). The losses occurred due to deliberate and sustained fraud perpetrated by Singapore-based trader Nick Leeson on his trading in the SIMEX exchange. Barings lost $1.5 billion because Nick Leeson took unauthorized futures and options positions on the Nikkei 225 and Japanese government bonds (JGBs) contracts. At the height of his activities, Leeson controlled 49 per cent of the open interest in the Nikkei 225 March 95 contract. Despite having to finance the margin calls as the market dropped, the

Barings board and senior management claim to have been unaware of Leeson's activities.

- In December 1993, Metallgesellschaft AG (MG) reported that its Energy Group was responsible for losses of approximately $1.5 billion, due mainly to cashflow problems resulting from large oil forward contracts it had written. MG used futures and swaps to hedge the fixed-rate oil products they had sold forward. While MG's hedge adequately transferred its market risk, the sheer size of their position (160 million barrels of oil) created an enormous amount of funding risk. When the oil prices started to drop, MG lost money on the hedge positions and received margin calls on their futures positions. Although gains in the forward contract positions offset the hedge losses, a negative cash flow occurred in the short run because no cash would be received for the gain in the value of the forward contracts until the oil was sold. Although no economic loss would occur because of their hedge strategy, the size of their position created a funding crisis that led to MG unwinding their positions and sustaining the $1.5 billion losses.

- On 26 September 1995 Daiwa Bank, one of Japan's major commercial banks, announced $1.1 billion in losses arising from the activities of a rogue trader at its New York branch. Iguchi Toshihide carried out more than 30,000 unauthorized trades over 11 years in US government bonds.

- In March 1997, Natwest Markets reported[2] that it had lost over £90 million due to mis-pricing of some OTC interest rate options. The mis-pricing had taken place over a period of two years. The fact that the problem remained undetected for such a long time brought into question the effectiveness of both internal and external controls at Natwest.

- Sumitomo's head copper trader, Yasuo Hamanaka, disguised losses totalling $1.8 billion over a ten year period. During that time, Hamanaka performed as much as $20 billion of unauthorized trades a year. He was able to hide his activities because he headed his section and had trade confirmations sent directly to himself, bypassing the back office.

- In December 1994, Orange County stunned the markets by announcing that its investment pool had suffered a loss of $1.6 billion.[3] This was the largest loss ever recorded by a local government investment pool, and led to the bankruptcy of the county shortly thereafter. This loss was the result of unsupervised investment activity of Bob Citron, the County Treasurer, who was entrusted with an $7.5 billion portfolio belonging to county schools, cities, special districts and the county itself. In times of fiscal restraints, Citron was viewed as a wizard who could painlessly deliver greater returns to investors. Indeed, Citron delivered returns about 2% higher than the comparable State pool. Citron was able to increase returns on the pool by investing in derivatives securities and leveraging the portfolio to the hilt. The pool was in such demand due to its track record that Citron had to turn down investments by agencies outside Orange County. Some local school districts and cities even issued short-term taxable notes to reinvest in the pool (thereby increasing their leverage even further). This was in spite of repeated public warnings, notably by John Moorlach, who ran for Treasurer in 1994, that the pool was too risky. Unfortunately, he was widely ignored and Bob Citron was re-elected. The investment strategy worked excellently until 1994, when the Fed started a series of interest rate hikes that caused severe losses to the pool. Initially, this was announced as a 'paper' loss. Shortly thereafter, the county declared bankruptcy and decided to liquidate the portfolio, thereby realizing the paper loss.

- In 1994, Procter and Gamble announced a $175m loss on leveraged derivatives. They had tried to save $1.5m of a total of $7.5m interest charge on a $200m loan. They had written a derivatives contract against the rise of American interest rates.

Every time the interest rates rose, the company decided to pursue the deal by increasing their exposure.

These are examples of just a few experiences over the past few years and there are many more reported and unreported incidents that could be added to the list. However, what is important is that none of these examples represent straight market or credit risk, but all are examples of a lack of procedures, systems or managerial control, i.e. these are all issues associated with operational risk.

Operational risk does not easily lend itself to quantification or standardization and therefore has received less attention from both the practitioners and regulators. In fact it has become a 'Cinderella' of the main risk categories within the industry, with relatively little investment in this area compared with market, counterparty or credit risk.

Collapse of Barings

The collapse of Barings brought into focus the issues of management and controls. The events that led to the collapse of Barings demonstrate how mismanagement and lack of controls can impact the operation – thus bringing down an institution with lightning speed. The control and risk management issues raised by Barings apply as much to cash positions as they do to derivative ones, but the leveraged nature of derivatives exaggerates any shortcomings in controls. With derivatives, only a relatively small amount of money (called a margin) is needed to establish a position, and an institution can find itself facing substantial financial obligations. The leverage and liquidity offered by major futures exchanges means that these obligations, once in place, can mount very quickly. This is where derivatives differ from bad loans or cash investments, whose ill-effects can take years to ruin an institution. Lillian Chew[4] reports that

The activities of Nick Leeson on the Japanese and Singapore futures exchanges, which led to the downfall of his employer, Barings, are well-documented. The main points are recounted here to serve as a backdrop to the main topic of this chapter – the policies, procedures and systems necessary for the prudent management of derivative activities. Barings collapsed because it could not meet the enormous trading obligations, which Leeson established in the name of the bank. When it went into receivership on February 27, 1995, Barings, through Leeson, had outstanding notional futures positions on Japanese equities and interest rates of US$27 billion: US$7 billion on the Nikkei 225 equity contract and US$20 billion on Japanese government bond (JGB) and Euroyen contracts. Leeson also sold 70,892 Nikkei put and call options with a nominal value of $6.68 billion. The nominal size of these positions is breathtaking; their enormity is all the more astounding when compared with the bank's reported capital of about $615 million.

The events that led to the collapse of Barings have been well documented. However, there are a number of key issues that need to be highlighted:

1 The major blame for collapse of Barings must lay with the attitude of the senior management to risk management and controls. There was only limited knowledge on derivatives among senior management. There was little analysis of how Leeson had been able to generate the reported profits. There was very little follow up of the audit recommendations. Senior management appeared almost negligent despite the fact that large sums of money were borrowed to cover the initial margin requirements. It is truly astounding that huge sums of money were remitted to Leeson without anyone requiring him to justify them.

2 Leeson was put in charge of both the front and the back office,

i.e. there was no segregation between these two key roles. The back office, through the process of recording, confirming, and settling the business transacted by the front office, provides the necessary checks to prevent unauthorized trading and minimize the risk of fraud. By putting him in charge of both the trading and the clearing and settlement functions, Barings provided Leeson with a perfect opportunity for systematic fraud and allowing him to suppress vital information about the true extent of his exposure.

3 There was no independent system of checking exposure and market risk. The senior management at Barings believed right to the end that Leeson had a hedged position and that there was no market risk. It was initial margin calls, i.e. funding risk, that eventually broke the bank. However, even if the bank had been able to fund the margin calls, it would not have been able to withstand the losses it would suffer on the expiry of the contracts.

4 There appeared to be no segregation of proprietary and client positions and there was no attempt at reconciling the reported size of the position and the requested funds to cover the margins.

5 Barings imposed no positional limits on Leeson's proprietary trading activity. While the nature of the arbitrage activities means that there is little price risk, there is still basis risk because the market movements may not be synchronized. Additionally, with no position limits, an institution can be open to funding risk where it is unable to meet its current liabilities due to cash flow problems. This was highlighted both in the case of Barings and Metallgesellschaft.

6 The technological, management or control infrastructure as well as the organizational culture within Barings were not conducive to effective risk management. The relatively small size of the bank made it unable to withstand the substantial losses that

it suffered. Barings' collapse was not due to derivatives but to lack of adequate risk management and control infrastructure and culture. However, what derivatives did was to expose these shortcomings to such an extent and with such speed that the management was unwilling or unable react to save the bank.

The derivative contracts (Nikkei 225) that brought about the downfall of Barings are among the simplest of derivative instruments. They are also the most transparent, since they are exchange traded contracts, with requirements for initial and variation margin. Despite this transparency, Leeson was able to build substantial position and during January and February 1995 alone, he asked for and received $835 million to cover in margin requirements. The senior managers at Barings assumed Leeson's positions were hedged. However, they did nothing about verifying this. They ignored the misgivings expressed by the auditors as well as the warning signals from internal and external sources.

The report[5] on the Barings' collapse prepared by the Board of Banking Supervision emphasized the serious lack of management awareness and control environments within Barings. These few extracts from the report highlight some of the issues:

> The Chairman of Barings plc, Peter Baring, described the failure of controls with regard to BFS as 'absolute'.

> We consider that those with direct executive responsibility for establishing effective controls must bear much of the blame. We identify below the ways in which, we have concluded, they failed to discharge this responsibility; and how others at lower levels of management were also at fault for failing to act effectively in relation to their own responsibilities.

> Leeson was not properly supervised.

> Leeson's back office functions were never effectively monitored; and to the extent that there were other staff in the back

office in Singapore they were relatively junior and it would seem, simply obeyed Leeson's instructions.

We concluded that the system of checks and balances necessary for the proper management and control of a financial institution failed in the case of Barings with regard to BFS in a most serious way, at a number of levels and in more than one location.

The Singapore authority's report on Barings is even more damming. It suggests that 'The Barings crash was a disaster waiting to happen. There were numerous instances when control at Barings broke down, from settlements to risk management to internal auditing. What struck you was the lack of communication and the lack of ability to use information coming from outside.'

A short extract from the concluding comments of the Lillian Chew report[4] provides the warning note for other institutions:

Although Barings' fate was only sealed in the final weeks of February, the seeds of its destruction were sown when senior management entered new businesses without ensuring adequate support and control systems. The collapse of Britain's oldest merchant bank was an extreme example of operations risk, i.e. the risk that deficiencies in information systems or internal controls result in unexpected loss. Will it happen again? Certainly, if senior managers of firms continue to disregard rules and recommendations which have been drawn up to ensure prudent risk-taking.

Notes

1 Ted Kim, *Force Majeure*, Futures and OTC World, November 1998, p. 25.
2 Financial Regulators to descend on Natwest, The *Irish Times* on the Web, March 3 1997.

3 Jorion Philippe, *Orange County Case: Using Value at Risk to Control Financial Risk*, 1998.
http://www.gsm.uci.edu/~jorion/oc/case.html.
4 Chew Lillian, How Leeson Broke Barings,
http://risk.ifci.ch/137560.htm.
5 *Report of the Board of Banking Supervision inquiry into the circumstances of the collapse of Barings*, Bank of England, HMSO 1995.

3 | Requirement for risk management

There is an absolute requirement to establish a risk strategy along with effective controls, procedures, processes and systems to monitor and manage risk. Operations and control functions may not be revenue earners, but they are at the core of the running of the business. If, or when, these controls fail then results can be spectacular, as happened in the case of Barings.

Whatever the image that operations conjures up, and in most cases it is not very complimentary, management is nevertheless as collectively responsible for its effective and efficient functioning as it is for maintaining the revenue streams and profit generated by the front office. Basic business sense would suggest that an inefficient or an ineffective back office would erode the profit made in the front office.

When it comes to derivatives, the importance and the effectiveness of the back office is highly significant. Derivatives, exchange traded or over the counter, have as their function the transfer of risk. The discipline associated with the clearing and settlement of these products is therefore of paramount importance if the use of the products is to be made safely.

The business managers responsible for the operations function have a duty to ensure that the necessary disciplines are successfully enforced. However the real key to a safe operation is the ability of the management generally to understand the processes and controls required for the settlement and administration of all the instruments involved. In most of the incidences where spectacular losses incurred due to derivatives activity, considerable sums of money were moving out of the organizations concerned.

This fact alone should have alerted the management to the impending problems. Leeson was a prime example of an individual exploiting the obvious lack of knowledge amongst his superiors at Barings.

The recent difficulties faced by the financial institutions have demonstrated the need for increased awareness of risks and enhanced levels of controls to manage that risk, particularly within the operational area.

Derivatives and risk management

The huge growth in the use of derivatives is primarily due to their role in managing and transferring market and credit risk. The power of derivatives lies in their versatility and universality; the makeup and characteristics of OTC derivatives are limited only by the analysts' creativity. Structure and payoff functions may be customized to fit a client's particular need, to offset existing risks or to gain exposure to desired risks. Unlike the products typical in the cash markets and on exchanges, OTC derivatives can be custom-tailored with unique structures and payoff functions that effectively dovetail with a client's particular risk profile and outlook.

However, like any complex tool, if these products are used in an uncontrolled fashion they can introduce further risk. For example, the collapse of Barings was due to a lack of internal control and management oversight. Derivatives re-allocate risk by the counterparty taking on the mirror position. However, depending on the type of derivative, their complexity and potential for large profits can lead their users to overlook the downside risks that remain.

Derivatives can be used to improve the allocation of resources and redistribute risks. Like other financial instruments, investors and borrowers employ derivatives for several purposes: as hedging tools for existing investments, to take speculative positions, to reduce borrowing costs, or simply as an outright asset investment to generate income.

Hedging existing positions

Many companies use derivatives to protect the value of an existing position to adverse market developments. The main use of derivatives is to hedge an asset against adverse price movements caused by market exposure to exchange rate or interest rate.

Reduce borrowing costs

By using interest rate swaps, borrowers can achieve lower borrowing costs where one party has a comparative borrowing advantage in one market and swaps payment streams with another counterparty that has a lower borrowing advantage in another market. The financing cost advantage is shared among the counterparties.

Investing to generate income

Derivatives offer a cheap and cost effective way of taking on new positions. For example, a company may buy a call option on an index instead of buying the composite shares and paying trading commissions. Additionally, if the institution wants exposure to new, volatile and less liquid market, the use of derivatives can be less complex than the traditional alternatives. Consider the example of an investment institution that wants to diversify its holdings across international borders. The traditional approach would be for the institution to buy foreign stocks – which would mean dealing in unfamiliar markets with potential high transaction costs and the additional complication of foreign currency exposures. However, using derivatives, the investment institution can purchase equity derivatives that provide a guaranteed principal and a yield tied to the dividends and price appreciation of the desired foreign securities. The institution gains a stake in the upside of foreign equities, limits its downside exposure, eliminates the necessity for transacting in foreign markets and avoids the high transaction costs of dealing in the cash markets. Thus the tailored derivative solution fits better and is more cost effective than the traditional approach.

Leverage, risks and volatility

The main difference between derivatives and other financial instruments is the leverage they offer. There is a greater amount of exposure for the same amount of committed capital. While the leverage in derivatives is what makes them cost-effective when covering existing exposures it is this same leverage that makes derivatives risky. While large gains from positive movements are obtainable, losses are also magnified. Consequently, the ability to leverage an investment to obtain greater returns is countered by the possibility of greater losses depending on the derivative and the nature of the position taken.

New derivatives products are being developed every day. There is increased interest in development of derivatives products such as hedges against insurance risks, e.g. hurricane futures and flood options. Catastrophe reinsurance futures are being traded on the Chicago Board of Trade, and OTC insurance derivatives are beginning to gain acceptance with users. Derivatives seem like the perfect solution for the insurance industry, whose capital base is increasingly stretched as the industry copes with the scale of potential catastrophic risks. As the derivative products develop, many companies will look to use derivatives to manage business risks, macroeconomics risks and insurance risks, as well as the traditional market and credit risks.

Despite the competitive benefits of derivatives as a risk management tool, some people remain fearful of them. The well-publicized losses in companies like Orange County, Barings, Diawa and

Sumitomo has created an impression that the instruments are inherently risky, complex and obscure.

The accelerating pace of change within the industry resulting from technological advances and the drive for globalization has highlighted the need for an approach to risk management that moves away from the current preoccupation with and excessive focus on administrative processes and controls. Organizations need to adopt strategies that take advantage of emerging technologies and organizational development techniques. What is needed is an approach to risk management that is inclusive, i.e. it addresses all the issues that impact an organization's ability to effectively manage risk. These include:

- risk appetite and risk management strategy

- development of risk management culture

- risk measurement and risk monitoring functions

- people, skills and training

- controls, policies and procedures

- technological infrastructure.

The problems throughout the 1990s have demonstrated that risk management approaches based on administrative controls have frequently broken down with disastrous results. In order to survive in the current environment, organizations need to focus on performance and results rather than tasks. It is only through effective integration of the corporate strategy, infrastructure, people and control systems that organizations can develop a risk-aware culture that will allow them to stay competitive and minimize the risk of financial disasters.

4 | Introduction to derivatives

Development of the derivatives industry

From very early times, and in many different trading environments, buyers and sellers have found it advantageous to enter into contracts, termed futures contracts, calling for a delivery of an underlying instrument or commodity at a later date.

Professor Don M. Chance in his article *Derivatives 'R' Us*[1] suggests that derivatives contracts are perhaps a lot older than is normally believed:

> Derivatives have a history much older than most people believe. In Genesis Chapter 29, around the year 1700 BC, Jacob purchased an option costing seven years labour that granted him the right to marry Laban's daughter Rachel. Laban reneged, however (perhaps the first default on an OTC contract) and forced Jacob to marry his older daughter Leah. Jacob did so but really loved Rachel so he purchased another option, requiring seven more years of labour, and finally married Rachel (bigamy was allowed). He ends up with two wives, twelve sons (patriarchs of the twelve tribes of Israel) and a lot of domestic friction, which is not surprising. Some argue that Jacob really had forward contracts, which obligated him to the marriages but that does not matter. Jacob did derivatives, one way or the other. Around 580 BC, Thales the Milesian purchased options on olive presses and made a fortune off of bumper crop in olives. So derivatives were around before the time of Christ.

Farmers and merchants have practised forward trading throughout the ages, seeking to hedge against uncertainties of demand, weather and harvest. The Dutch whalers in the sixteenth century, for example, entered into forward sales contracts before sailing, partly to finance their voyage and partly to get a better price for their product. With the advent of fast transatlantic Cunard mail service in 1840, the Liverpool cotton importers entered into forward contracts with the US exporters who were able to send samples to Liverpool in advance of the slow cargo ships. The first 'futures' contracts are generally traced to the Yodoya rice market in Osaka, Japan around 1650. These were standardized contracts, which made them much like today's futures, although it is not known if the contracts were marked to market daily. Forward trading of this sort in grains, coffee, rice and other commodities occurred in many centres in the USA, Europe and Asia between the seventeenth and the middle of the nineteenth century.

However, futures trading in commodities is fundamentally different in two main ways.

- Where as forwards trading involves individual negotiated contracts between two counterparties, futures trading is based on standardized contracts.

- The existence of the clearing house as a counterpart to both sides of the trade that not only settles the trade but also assumes counterparty risk means that for the first time it was no longer necessary for mutual familiarity between parties doing business.

The next major event in the development of the derivatives markets was the creation of the Chicago Board of Trade (CBOT) in 1848. Due to its prime location on Lake Michigan, Chicago was developing as a major centre for the storage, sale and distribution of grain for the outlying territories. There were severe strains on Chicago's storage facilities following the harvest, and under utilization at other times. Additionally the farmers and merchants wanted to hedge against the large fluctuations in the spot price of the grain. This led to the creation of the 'to-arrive' contracts enabling the farmers to get a better price for their products and merchants to avoid serious price risk. As these contracts evolved they became standardized with respect to size, grade and delivery period. Once established the standardization enabled contracts to be readily traded. Thus the forerunner of today's markets was born and farmers or merchants who wanted to hedge against price fluctuations, caused by poor or bumper harvests, bought and sold contracts with traders (or market makers) who were willing to make a different price for buying and selling. Speculators, who wanted to gamble on the price going up or down without actually buying or selling the physical grain themselves, were also attracted to the market. Therefore liquidity in the contracts was created. The trader was able to lay off the risk he had assumed from buying and selling with the hedgers, by doing the opposite buying and selling with the speculators. The trader's profit was the difference between buying and selling the contracts. The introduction of the clearing house more or less completed the initial development of the futures markets.

In 1874 the Chicago Mercantile Exchange's (CME) predecessor, the Chicago Produce Exchange, was formed, which provided the market for perishable agricultural products like butter and eggs. In 1919 it was recognized and became the modern day Mercantile Exchange. Futures on a variety of commodities have since come to the exchange, including pork bellies, hogs and cattle.

The early decades of the twentieth century saw a significant growth in the futures industry but there were very few further developments outside the traditional commodities contracts.

However following the collapse of the Bretton Woods system of fixed exchange rates in 1971, the CME set up a new exchange called the International Monetary Market (IMM) that would trade British pounds, Canadian dollars, German marks, Italian lira, Japanese yen, Mexican pesos and Swiss francs against the US dollar. These were the first futures contracts that were not based on physical commodities.

In 1975 the Chicago Board of Trade created the first interest rate futures contract, one based on Ginnie Mae (GNMA) mortgages. While the contract met with initial success, it eventually died. In 1975 the CME responded with the 90-day Treasury bill futures contract. In 1977 the CBOT created the 30-year T-bond futures contract, which went on to be the highest volume contract. In 1982 the CME created the Eurodollar contract, which has gone on to become incredibly active, surpassing T-bonds in terms of dollar amount traded. A flood of contracts spanning the yield curve was launched by a number of exchanges in the early 1980s and cash settlement was introduced as an alternative to physical delivery.

There were two crucial developments that occurred in the derivatives market in the early 1980s. The first was the launch of currency options by the Philadelphia Stock Exchange in 1983. While equity options had been available in the US, it was the currency options and futures options that instigated the development of a whole generation of risk management techniques and strategies. The second was the advent of the first currency swap in 1981 followed by interest rate swap in 1982. These over-the-counter (OTC) products paved the way for the development of a parallel market to the exchange-traded markets.

By the mid-1980s, futures, options, swaps and forward rate agreements (FRAs) had revolutionized financial risk management. Trading volumes increased and derivatives exchanges sprung up around the globe: the New York Futures Exchange in 1980, the London International Financial Futures and Options Exchange (LIFFE) in 1982, the Singapore International Monetary Exchange (SIMEX) in 1983 and Marche a Terme International de France (MATIF) added financial futures to the French market in 1985.

At the same time, the development of the OTC market added an array of new products that can be customized to suit almost any risk/reward profile. Swaps, options, swaptions, caps and floors can now be bought from market makers and brokers on financials, equities, commodities and metals.

Nowadays, financial futures products dominate trading over the more traditional commodities contracts world-wide.

The other half of the organized derivatives market is the options contract. Like futures contracts, options trading can also be traced back to the Middle Ages. However, it was not until the creation of the Chicago Board of Options (CBOE) Exchange in 1973 that the 'traded options' were born. You could trade stock options in standardized contracts on an organized exchange where the performance of the contract on exercise was guaranteed.

Since then option markets have grown in the US and globally. Like futures markets they cover a wide range of products, including options on futures. Although options have been trading for a shorter time than futures they are nevertheless extremely popular with both hedgers and speculators alike.

The 1980s and 1990s have seen a tremendous growth in the futures options markets throughout the world. The London International Financial Futures and Options Exchange (LIFFE) which opened for business in 1982 has led the European challenge to the dominance of the Chicago exchanges.

Other futures and options markets followed, notably the Singapore International Monetary Exchange in 1984 and the Hong Kong Futures Exchange in 1985. Many new markets in the Americas, Europe and the Far East followed these during the late 1980s and early 1990s.

Other major exchanges include:

- Marche a Terme International de France (MATIF) in France, opened in 1986

- Deutsche Terminborse (DTB) in Germany, opened in 1990

- Osterreichische Termin- und Optionenborse (OTOB) in Austria, opened in 1991

- Bolsa de Mercadorias and Futuros (BM&F) in Brazil, opened 1991

- During 1996 exchanges opened in Kuala Lumpur and Portugal.

Today, the futures and options industry is truly global. Table 4.1 shows the top futures exchanges in 1998.

Table 4.1 Top futures exchanges by volume of contracts traded.[1]

Position	Exchange
1	CBOT, USA
2	EUREX, Germany & Switzerland
3	CME, USA
4	CBOE, USA
5	LIFFE, UK
6	AMEX, USA
7	NYMEX, USA
8	BM&F, Brazil
9	Amsterdam Ex., Netherlands
10	PSX, USA

The international futures exchanges have seen massive growth over the last few years; the over-the-counter (OTC) markets have seen an equally significant increase in business. The advent of the first currency swap in 1981, followed by the first interest rate swap less than a year later marked the beginning of the era of swaps and OTC derivatives. By the end of the 1980s, a whole range of OTC derivative products including swaps, forwards, options, cap and floor were available for trading or risk management purposes.

The International Swaps and Derivatives Association's (ISDA) preliminary data for its 1996 market survey indicated that the combined notional amount of globally outstanding interest rate swaps, currency swaps and interest rate options transactions stood at $24.292 trillion on 31 December 1996, compared with $17.713 trillion on the same day a year earlier.

The volume of business in both exchange traded and over-the-counter continues to grow with new exchanges and new products providing users with the medium to control and transfer risk.

Understanding derivatives products

There is a great perception that derivatives are very complex and only understood by the very few 'rocket scientists' who put the products together. Of course there are some very complex derivatives products but these only account for a very small fraction of the total exposure. Even these can be broken down into their much simpler constituent products – which is exactly what the institutions that offer them do in order to manage the risk of such products. The building blocks of these complex derivatives are hardly new; the forward contracts, which allow the user to lock in the future price, have been with us for hundreds of years. Options, which are the other main building block, are somewhat more complicated but again hardly new; options were traded in the seventeenth century in Amsterdam.

Before discussing derivatives products in detail, it is useful to review some of the cash products that they are based on. All derivatives are based on some underlying cash product. These 'cash' products are:

- **Spot foreign exchange.** This is the buying and selling of foreign currency at the exchange rates that you see quoted on the news. As these rates change between the various currencies, you make or lose money.

- **Commodities.** These include grain, pork bellies, coffee beans, orange juice, etc.

- **Equities** (termed 'stocks' in the US). This is the buying and selling of shares in companies quoted on the various exchanges.

- **Bonds.** There are many different varieties of bonds, e.g. Eurobonds, domestic bonds, fixed interest/floating rate notes, etc. Bonds are medium- to long-term negotiable debt securities issued by governments, government agencies, supra-national organizations such as the World Bank, and companies. Negotiable means that they may be freely traded without reference to the issuer of the security. Bonds are referred to as debt securities because, in the event of the company going bankrupt, the bond-holders will be repaid their debt in full before the holders of unsecuritized debt get any of their money back.

- **Short-term and medium-term debt securities.** These are debt instruments such as T-bills (issued by governments), commercial paper (issued by companies) or certificates of deposits (CDs). While there is no defined period for these, the short-term instruments are mainly less than one year in maturity; 'medium term' is commonly taken to mean form one to five years in maturity, and 'long term' anything above that.

- **Over-the-counter ('OTC') money market instruments.** These are products such as such as loans/deposits that are based upon borrowing or lending. They are contracts between the two counterparties making the trade.

Derivative products are contracts that have been constructed based on one of the 'cash' products described above. Examples of these products include options, futures, forwards, swaps, forward rate agreements (FRAs) etc.

Futures contracts

A futures contract is a standardized agreement between two parties that commits one to sell and the other to buy a stipulated quantity and grade of a commodity, currency, security, index or other specified item at a set price on or before a given date in the future. These contracts have several key features:

- The buyer of a futures contract agrees to receive delivery and the seller of a futures contract agrees to make delivery.

- The contracts are traded on exchanges, either by open outcry in specified trading areas (called pits or rings) or electronically via a computerized network.

- Futures contracts are marked to market each day at their end-of-day settlement prices.

- Futures contracts can be terminated by an offsetting transaction (i.e. an equal and opposite transaction to the one that opened the position) executed at any time prior to the contract's expiration. The vast majority of futures contracts are terminated by offset or a final cash payment rather than by delivery.

A standardized futures contract has specific characteristics. These include:

- Underlying instrument – the commodity, currency, financial instrument or index upon which the contract is based.

- Size – the amount of the underlying item covered by the contract.

- Delivery cycle – the specified months for which contracts can be traded.

- Expiration date – the date by which a particular futures trading month ceases to exist and therefore all obligations under it must terminate.

- Grade or quality specification and delivery location – a detailed description of the commodity, security or other item that is being traded and, as permitted by the contract, a specification of items of higher or lower quality or of alternate delivery locations available at a premium or discount.

- Settlement mechanism – the terms of the physical delivery of the underlying item or of a terminal cash payment.

The mechanics of futures trading are straightforward: both buyers and sellers deposit funds called margin with either a clearing house or with a brokerage firm. This amount is typically a small percentage – less than 10 per cent – of the total value of the item underlying the contract.

Figure 4.1(a) provides the payoff characteristic of a 'long' futures contract, i.e. if you buy (go long) a futures contract and the price goes up, the profit is the amount of the price increase times the contract size; and if the price goes down, you lose an amount equal to the price decrease times the contract size.

Figure 4.1(b) provides the payoff characteristic of a 'short' futures contract, i.e. if you sell (go short) a futures contract and the price

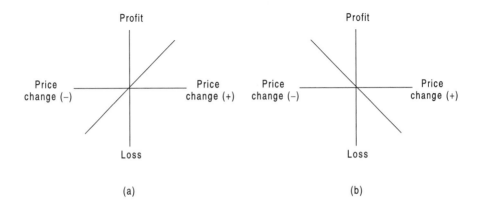

Figure 4.1 Payoff for futures position: (a) long futures position, (b) short futures position.

Understanding derivatives products

goes down, the profit is the amount of the price decrease times the contract size; and if the price goes up, you lose an amount equal to the price increase times the contract size.

Options contracts

An option is, for its owner, the right but not the obligation, to buy specified number of underlying futures contracts or a specified amount of a commodity, currency, index or financial instrument at specified price on or before a given future date. The owner pays

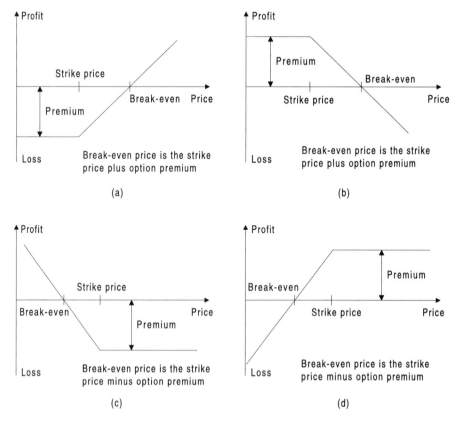

Figure 4.2 Payoff profiles and break-even analysis for options positions: (a) call buyer, (b) call seller, (c) put buyer, (d) put seller.

a premium for this right. Since the buyer of the option has the right to purchase, while the seller has the obligation to sell (if the buyer wishes), the payoff profiles for the two parties are quite different (see Figure 4.2). There are two types of options: call options and put options. A call option gives the buyer the right, but not the obligation, to purchase the underlying contract at a specified price (the strike or exercise price) during the life of the option. A put option gives the buyer the right, but not the obligation, to sell the underlying contract at the strike or exercise price before the option expires. As with futures, exchange-traded options positions can be closed out by offset, i.e. execution of a trade of equal size on the other side of the market from the transaction that originated the position. Figure 4.2 examines the payoff profiles and break-even points for each of the four basic options positions. A long position in an option gives you unlimited profit and a limited loss potential (the premium). A short position in the option results in a limited profit (the premium) and an unlimited loss potential.

The major difference between futures and options arises from the different obligations of an option's buyer and seller. A futures contract requires both buyer and seller to perform the contract, either by an offsetting transaction or by delivery, and both parties to a futures contract derive a profit or loss equal to the difference between the price when the contract was initiated and when it was terminated. An option buyer, however, is not obliged to fulfil the option contract. The option buyer's loss is limited to the premium paid, but in order for the buyer to make a profit, the price must increase above (for call option) or decrease below (for put option) the option's strike price by the amount of the premium paid. The option seller (writer or grantor), who has received the premium received, is obliged to fulfil the option contract if the buyer chooses to exercise the option. The option exercise only takes place if the option is 'in the money' before it expires.

The value of an option has two components, i.e. intrinsic value and time value. The intrinsic value of the option is the difference between the strike price and the price of the underlying instrument. The time value of the option depends on the time to expiry, volatility and interest rates. In general terms, the longer the option has to run and higher the volatility, the more the time value of the option.

Options are traded on both the organized exchanges and on the OTC markets. Options products include currency options, equity options, bond options, options on futures, etc.

Forward contracts

Forward contracts are individual agreements between counterparties to trade an asset at a specified date in the future for an agreed price. Forward contracts are generally traded on the OTC markets. Historically, forward contracts developed as customized instruments involving delivery of an underlying commodity or financial instrument.

Forward contracts have a number of characteristics that distinguish them from futures contracts. The most important of these is that forward contracts are negotiated between two counterparties who can customize the underlying asset and delivery location and dates, to meet their own requirements. Unlike the futures contracts where the contract performance is guaranteed by the clearing house, there is no such guarantor for the forward contracts. The counterparties have direct credit exposure with each other.

A forward contract can be considered as a customized futures contract. A forward is an agreement between two parties to buy or sell a commodity or asset at a specific future time for an agreed upon price. Typically, the contract is between a producer and a merchant; two financial institutions; or a financial institution and a corporate client. There are a number of important distinctions between forward and futures contracts and these include:

- The performance of exchange traded futures contracts is guar-

anteed by the clearing house of the exchange on which the contracts were traded. The forward contracts, on the other hand,
are individually negotiated between two counterparties.
Therefore issues associated with credit risk need to be
addressed.

- Unlike the exchange-traded contracts that require daily payments of profits and losses via a mark-to-market margining
system, the forward contracts generally do not involve daily or
other periodic payments of accumulated gains or losses. As a
result of this there is a potential for large paper profit and
losses to accumulate with forward contracts. This can increase
the likelihood and cost of default. Counterparties need to
establish procedures to mitigate this increased credit risk.
Depending upon the creditworthiness of the counterparties and
the magnitude of the exposure, parties to forward contracts
may be required to post collateral or make periodic payments
against accumulated losses.

- Exchange traded derivatives contracts are standardized with
defined characteristics; forward contracts are created on a customized basis, with terms such as the grade of the underlying
commodity or asset, delivery location and date, credit arrangements and default provisions negotiated between and tailored
to the needs of the two parties.

- In the absence of standardized contracts and a large number of
buyers and sellers, forward markets often lack the low transaction costs and ease of entry and exit found on liquid exchange
markets.

Forward rate agreements (FRAs)

An FRA is a contract between two parties that fixes the rate of
interest on a notional amount of principle (loan or deposit) for an
agreed future lending period starting from an agreed settlement

date. The two parties to the FRA contract agree to exchange the difference between the market rate of interest and a prearranged fixed interest rate on the contract settlement date on an agreed notional amount. The terms of the contract include:

- the notional amount of principal;

- settlement date, i.e. the date from which the rate is fixed;

- the term of the contract;

- contract interest rate.

If an institution wishes to fix the future borrowing costs, it can buy an FRA. If the interest rate raises, it will receive a compensatory payment under the FRA contract that will reflect the increased cost of borrowing. If a company wishes to fix the rate of return on a future investment, it can sell an FRA. If the interest rate falls, it will receive a compensatory payment to reflect its reduced income due to the falling interest rates. However, in return for removing the short term interest rate risk, the company gives up the potential benefit of any favourable interest rate movements.

The formula for calculating the compensatory payments is:

$$\frac{A * (L - F) * D}{B + L * D}$$

Where:

A = Notional contract amount
L = Market interest rate expressed as a percentage value and not a whole number (e.g. for a LIBOR of 9 per cent L = 0.09)
F = The FRA fixed interest rate expressed as a percentage value and not a whole number (e.g. for a FRA rate of 7 per cent F = 0.07)
D = Time period for the FRA in days
B = Basis for interest calculation, 360 or 365.

An FRA can be used to hedge short-term interest rate exposure by locking future interest rates for borrowing or investing. As there is no exchange of principal, the credit risk for an FRA is confined to the non-payment of the amounts based on the rate differentials between the market rate and the FRA rate.

Swaps

A swap is a transaction whereby two counterparties establish a tailored bilateral agreement to exchange cash flows at periodic intervals during the life of the deal according to a prearranged formula. The cash flows are based on notional principal amount of the swap. In most cases, such as with an interest rate swap, this notional amount never changes hands but is used as a reference point for calculating future cash flows. The most common form of swap is a 'vanilla' interest rate swap. With that structure, one party pays interest at a fixed rate while the other pays according to a floating rate such as LIBOR (London inter-bank offered rate). Payments are based upon a specified notional amount and are netted against each other. Payments will be made at a fixed interval (e.g. semi-annually or annually) for the life of the swap. A number of important characteristics of a swap are illustrated by looking at the interest rate swap:

- Only the interest payments are exchanged, the principal amount is not. This has important implications when calculating credit exposure for a swap.

- One party pays the fixed rate while the other pays the floating rate. LIBOR is the most commonly used floating rate index.

- The swaps contract defines the notional amount, maturity, floating rate to be used as well as the fixed rate (i.e. swap rate).

Since swaps are OTC products whose characteristics can be tailored to meet the exact needs of the users, there are many different types of swaps. These include:

- **Currency swap** – This involves one party making payments in one currency and another party makes payments in another currency.

- **Commodity swap** – This is when one party makes a set of payments based on the price of a commodity, such as gold, and the other party makes payments based on fixed or on some other floating rate or price.

- **Equity swap** – An equity swap involves one party paying the other a rate based on the rate of return on an equity index. The S&P 500 or FTSE are examples of these indexes. The second party might make payment based on something else. This party may make the payment based on a fixed rate such as LIBOR, or another equity index.

- **Basis swap** – The basis swap is a swap between two floating rate indices. For example interest payments based on LIBOR may be exchanged for interest payments based on the commercial paper index on the same notional amount.

- **Amortizing swap** – This is where the notional amount starts at a high level and gradually decreases. Accreting swap is where the notional amount starts low and gradually increase during the life of the swap.

Since they are OTC instruments, swaps are not guaranteed by any clearing houses. As a consequence, only highly rated corporations have access to the swaps market.

There is a whole plethora of OTC derivatives products that are continuously being developed. These include caps, floors, collars, swaptions and hybrid derivatives. Since individuals can 'create' OTC derivative products by means of an agreement, the types of derivative products that can be developed are limited only by the human imagination. Therefore, there is no definitive list of OTC products.

Product comparisons

There a number of common characteristics between exchange traded futures and options, equities, forward contracts and over-the-counter (OTC) derivatives. However, there are some substantial differences between the products as well. A comparison of the products highlights some of the issues.

Futures, options and securities

There are some critical differences between derivatives and the equity products. The leveraged nature of the derivatives products means that a relatively small capital outlay allows the investor to gain a substantial exposure in the market. This characteristic, along with the flexibility of the OTC products, makes derivatives such an efficient hedging and risk management. However, there are a number of other important differences between derivatives and equities. These differences include:

- Although investment products can be used in a speculative manner, the main use of derivatives (both exchange traded and OTC products) is to manage and transfer risk. The principal purpose of equities markets is to foster capital formation.

- In futures trading there is a short for every long; in equities markets, short positions are normally a minor factor. In addition, establishing a short position in a futures market is no more difficult than establishing a long position. In contrast, a short position in equities requires owning or borrowing the securities and payment of dividends.

- The margin deposited by the customer for futures trading is termed the performance bond or good faith money, securing the promise to fulfil the contract's obligations. The futures positions are marked to market on a daily basis. In margined stock purchases, the margin acts as a down payment, and the balance of the purchase price is borrowed, with interest charged. There is no daily marking to market in the equities markets, but if prices change by a significant amount a maintenance margin call is made.

- The life of a futures contract is limited to its specified expiration date. Most equities, on the other hand, are issued without a termination date.

- A price limit on a futures contract establishes the maximum range of trading prices during a given day. A futures position limit establishes the maximum exposure a market participant may assume in a particular market. Many futures markets have price and/or position limits. Equities typically do not have limits on price movements or the size of positions.

- While the outstanding number of equities is fixed at a given moment, there is no theoretical limit on the number of derivatives that may exist at a particular time in a specific market.

- For equities, a customer can ask for a certificate that provides evidence of ownership. There is no comparable certificate for futures and options. A customer's written record of a futures position is the trade confirmation received from the brokerage house through which the trade was made.

- The open-outcry futures markets typically operate with a multiple market-maker system, involving floor traders and floor brokers competing on equal footing in an auction-style, open-outcry market. Equities markets typically operate with a specialist system, where the designated specialist has specified privileges and responsibilities with respect to a given stock, although non-specialist brokers may also compete for trades.

Exchange-traded versus OTC products

There are two markets for trading derivatives products, namely organized exchanges e.g. CBOT, LIFFE etc., and the over-the-counter market. It is important to understand their characteristics. The characteristics of exchange-traded derivatives are:

- organized market with contract terms and specifications clearly stated in the rules;

- clearing organization guaranteeing the fulfilment of the contracts;

- standardized contracts;

- secondary market facilitating trading;

- liquidity;

- flex contracts (exchange traded with flexible terms);

- availability of prices for valuation.

The characteristics of OTC derivatives are:

- not traded on an organized market;

- offered direct to counterparty;

- no guarantor to ensure fulfilment of contract;

- no secondary market to facilitate trading;

- direct counterparty risk;

- flexible products designed to meet specific requirements;

- no public price source to enable easy valuation;

- potential liquidity problems.

There are growing number of products available on the exchanges around the world. The exchanges are providing additional flexibility, through products like the flex options, to meet the challenge of the OTC markets. Unlike the OTC instruments, there is a definitive list of all the contracts that are traded on the various exchanges around the world. Table 4.2 gives the most successful contracts in 1998.

The exchanges are continuously developing new products. Flex options are the latest in line of new contracts that are a cross between OTCs and exchange traded products. The advantage of flex options is that participants can choose various parts of the contract specification such as the expiry date and exercise price.

Table 4.2 The top exchange traded contracts[3]

Rank	Contract	Exchange	Country
1	UST-Bond	CBOT	USA
2	3-month Eurodollar	CME	USA
3	BUND	Eurex	Germany
4	3-Month Euromark	LIFFE	UK
5	US T-Bond options	CBOT	USA
6	Interest rate	BM&F	Brazil
7	3-month Sterling	LIFFE	UK
8	S&P 100 Index option	CBOE	USA
9	3-month Eurodollar option	CME	USA
10	BOBL	Eurex	Germany

Understanding the market structures

This section looks primarily at how the structure of the markets for trading exchange traded derivative (ETD) products. An exchange is the place where futures and options are traded by members (corporates or individuals) who carry out their business under the rules and regulations of the exchange. The exchange in turn is subject to regulation by the domestic government agencies.

The debate about which trading method, open outcry or electronic trading, has been raging for the last few years and the argument now appears to be tilting towards electronic trading. Since the largest exchanges in the world, i.e. CBOT and CME are open outcry, most of the trading is still done on the floor of the exchange using this method. Electronic trading systems are becoming more established with virtually all the new exchanges adopting this method of trading. Even the open outcry exchanges are using electronic trading systems to supplement the more traditional trading method. LIFFE has recently decided to list all its products on an electronic platform and now offers both electronic trading as well as floor trading facilities.

In light of the organizational and technological changes that have taken place over the past few years, and the global nature of the financial markets, it is surprising to note that the majority of the futures and options business still takes place on the floor of exchanges. In the futures exchanges, where the total dollar volume of all futures contracts world-wide is over $500 billion[4] a day, traders still meet in designated locations (the trading pit) and buy and sell products by a combination of shouting and hand signals. The process is known as open outcry, or pit trading or floor trading. Figure 4.3 shows the trading volumes for open outcry and electronic exchanges.[5]

Whatever the trading mechanism, the exchange plays a key role in

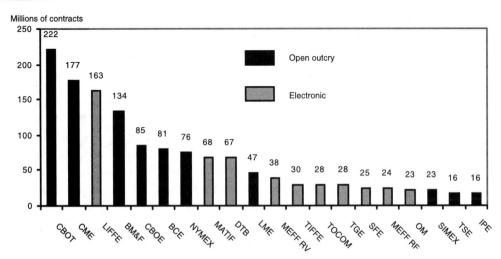

Figure 4.3 Trading volumes for open outcry and electronic exchanges.

the trading process. The exchange, through its clearing house, acts as the counterparty to every transaction and provides the systems for the clearing and settlement of the contracts.

Impact of technology

Whatever the trading mechanism offered by the exchanges, technology has an ever-increasing role in this environment. For example, the client enters the trade on a computer in their office; this is automatically routed to the broker's booth on the exchange floor; the trader in the pit is informed through his headset; he executes the trade on the floor and enters the details on his electronic pad; the information is routed to the clearing house, price vendors and the trade confirmed back to the client.

There is an increasing amount of technology on the trading floors. CBOT's[6] trading facility includes 12,000 computers, 6,000 voice devices and 2,000 video devices all linked together with 27,000 miles of cable.

Despite all this technology, open outcry exchanges are under increasing pressure to move to electronic trading. In Europe, the battle for market share is at its fiercest between LIFFE, which has traditionally operated open outcry, and Eurex, which is the largest electronic exchange. The Eurex exchange was created by the merger between Deutsche Terminborse (DTB) and the Swiss Options and Financial Futures Exchange (SOFFEX). The battle in Europe, at least, has been won by electronic trading with LIFFE and MATIF both moving to electronic trading.

As the derivatives market becomes global, exchanges are linking together in order to list their most successful products on mutually beneficial exchanges. There has been evidence of this recently with LIFFE listing the Euroyen contract (also traded on TIFFE) and the Japanese Government Bond (also traded on TSE). Both contracts are cleared by the Japanese exchanges with open positions being passed over at the close of business in London. There is continuing developments between the major exchanges to list each other's products in the various time zones.

The structure and the rules vary from exchange to exchange. The regulatory environment is dependent on the country where the exchange is based.

Structure of the exchanges

The board of directors, who have responsibility for the management of exchange, is elected from a representative cross-section of the membership of the exchange. The board works through their appointed practitioner committees who consider specific issues which are relevant to the day-to-day operation of the exchange. These issues typically concern floor trading, product development, membership and rules and default and risk management.

Each exchange has a membership that is normally drawn from all parts of the financial services industry. LIFFE's membership originates from many countries but a lot of exchanges have a mostly domestic membership.

Membership is generally broken down into two categories, non-clearing and clearing. Non-clearing membership is for companies who only wish to execute business on the exchange. This is further broken down into companies who only execute business for themselves, also known as proprietary traders or locals, and companies who execute client business as well as their own. Clearing members are companies who execute business, in any capacity, but also clear or settle that business with the exchange or clearing house. Again this is broken down into two further categories; those companies who only clear their own business and those who clear other non-clearing members' business as well as their own.

Most exchanges issue *seats* that entitle the holder to execute business on the exchange and, in certain cases, carry voting rights.

These seats or trading permits can be purchased from the exchange or can be leased from other member firms depending on availability. Also, most exchanges issue various trading permits that are specific to different products.

The operational expenses of exchanges are funded by exchange levies or fees on all contracts traded. The membership fees charged for trading permits provide additional income.

Table 4.3 Exchange seat prices[7]

Exchange	Last sale	Year ago
AMEX	$405,000	$405,000
CBOE	$460,000	$725,000
CBOT	$450,000	$775,000
CME	$301,000	$425,000
COMEX	$62,000	$91,000
CSCE	$110,000	$160,000
IPE	£100,000	£110,000
KCBT	$70,500	$64,000
LIFFE	£60,000	£155,000
NYCE	$81,000	$650,000
NYMEX	$500,000	$84,000
Pacific SE	$365,000	$310,000
PHLX	$175,500	$190,500

LIFFE is a good example of an exchange with a diverse membership. It has approximately 200 member companies. Over 70 per cent of these are foreign owned.

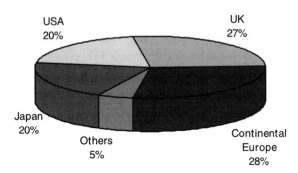

Figure 4.4 Geographical origin of LIFFE's membership.[8]

Role of the clearing house

Clearing houses provide a range of services related to guarantee of contracts, clearance and settlement of trades and management of risk for their members and associated exchanges. The clearing houses can be organized in a wide variety of forms: some are departments within their affiliated exchanges, others are independent legal entities. Some clearing houses provide services to only one exchange; others serve a group of exchanges. Some clearing houses are owned by their member clearing firms, others are owned by exchanges or are public corporations. However, despite these organizational differences, there are a number of common features that are functions of all clearing houses. The most important of these features is, with very few exceptions, that clearing houses act as the central counterparty to deals struck between exchange members, i.e. the clearing house becomes the buyer to every seller of a contract and the seller to every buyer.

As central counterparty to trades on the exchange, the clearing house is exposed to counterparty risks and it must establish procedures to control those risks. A basic risk control mechanism is restriction of access to the clearing process. Clearing members typically are a subset of the exchange members that must meet defined financial and operating standards. This structure of clearing houses creates the need for intermediary relationships between various participants in the clearing process; non-clearing members must arrange for a clearing firm to assume financial responsibility for their trades. The clearing house has a principal-to-principal relationship with its members; the clearing house typically asserts that it has no legal relationship with the clients of its member clearing firms, including those clients that are exchange members.

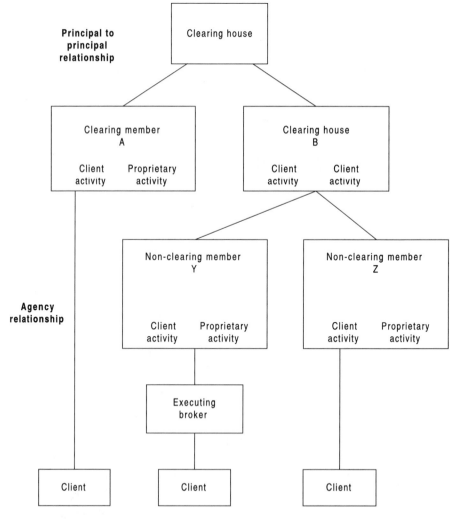

Figure 4.5 Clearing house and its counterparties.

Clearing members and their clients

Clearing members serve as intermediaries in their provision of clearing services to clients, which may include non-clearing exchange members or individuals or firms that are not members of the exchange.

Where a non-member of the exchange originates the trade, the clearing of that trade can take place through different paths. The retail client might choose to have the trade executed and cleared through the same institution. Alternatively, the client may have its trades executed through one member but use a different institution as the clearing broker. The executing broker would then give-up the trade to the selected clearing member. In this way the client may execute the trades through many brokers, but choose to clear through a single entity to provide enhanced risk management and control.

OTC derivatives clearing and settlement process

Unlike exchange traded derivatives, OTC derivatives are privately negotiated transactions between two counterparties that typically are executed by telephone. These contracts are traded internationally by dealers to end-users and other dealers. The relationship between the counterparties is exclusively principal-to-principal. Brokers may be used to locate counterparties, but the brokers are not themselves counterparties to the transactions. The dealers tend to be large international financial institutions. End-users include banks, insurance companies, pension funds, other financial institutions, non-financial corporations, governments, supranational entities (e.g. the World Bank) and high-net-worth individuals. The counterparties bilaterally negotiate the economic and credit terms of the transactions. Although the documentation tends to be standardized in many respects, important aspects of both the economic and the credit terms can be customized. The transactions are confirmed and settled bilaterally between the counterparties.

These characteristics of OTC derivatives distinguish them from exchange-traded derivatives that are transacted on a central trading floor or through an electronic trading system and are cleared and settled centrally through a clearinghouse, which acts as central counterparty to all the contracts. The economic terms of exchange-traded contracts, i.e. underlying assets, value, delivery dates and strike prices (for options), and credit terms are standardized. This standardization and the creation of a central counterparty make the contracts more liquid than OTC derivatives.

Transaction processing and settlement for OTC instruments

The operations function, which is responsible for transaction processing and settlement, performs a key role in managing risk. It minimizes credit, market and legal risks by ensuring that all transactions are accurately recorded in internal systems, that the details of trades are agreed as soon as possible after execution with the counterparty and any disagreements resolved, and that the firm's settlement obligations are met when they fall due. Operations risk is minimized by automating, as far as possible, all the process from trade execution through to confirmation and settlement. This reduces the errors due to manual intervention during confirmation and settlement of OTC derivatives transactions. While it is possible to automate the processing of plain vanilla transactions, more complex OTC transactions require significant manual intervention at many stages of the processing.

Trade execution

Most OTC derivatives transactions are executed by telephone although automated brokerage systems are used for certain foreign exchange derivatives. Traders are responsible for ensuring that trades fall within credit lines for the counterparty and overall trading limits. While some institutions are beginning to develop integrated credit management systems that provide online access showing the availability of credit lines for counterparties, others need to apply to a credit or risk control function before executing the trade in order to ensure that limits are not breached.

Although brokers are used in some transactions, they never act as principals in OTC markets. They merely help locate and bring together the counterparties willing to transact the business.

Data capture

After executing the trade, the details, including the date, time, counterparty name, instrument, payment dates, etc. are recorded. Trade data is either input directly into a front office processing system by the traders and fed electronically to the operations area, or recorded on tickets and passed to operations for manual entry into the processing system.

Confirmation processing

After a trade has been executed, the counterparties confirm its details to each other in order to produce an agreed record of the transaction. There is increased use of the confirmation templates developed by ISDA for standard trades. However, bespoke templates may be used for some more complicated products. The confirmation lists all the economic terms, e.g. the notional amount, effective date, rates and payment dates, and legal terms of the trade. When a firm receives a confirmation, it typically checks all the terms against its own confirmation. Any discrepancy between the two has to be reconciled and the confirmations reissued for signature by both counterparties.

Confirmations are normally prepared by the back office staff who are independent of the traders in the front office. Legal as well as operational staff may be involved, particularly for more complex products or if the firm does not already have a signed master agreement with the counterparty.

There are standard SWIFT messages for confirmations of foreign currency options, FRAs, interest rate swaps and cross-currency swaps. In practice, SWIFT is used by dealers principally for confirming FRAs and foreign currency options. There are very few organizations that have automated links between their OTC derivatives back office and their connection to the SWIFT system. SWIFT can be used only for confirming trades with other SWIFT members.

Management information and internal controls

An institution's ability to measure, monitor and control credit risks and market risks is critically dependent on timely and accurate data capture and reporting. Where there is an automatic feed of data from the front office into the operational and risk management systems, accurate management reports can be available in real time. Often trades are manually input into to the operational and risk management systems from deal tickets that are generated at the end of the day. Management reports are then only available once a day (usually in the morning, before trading starts, reflecting the previous day's trades). Additionally, market risk and credit risk systems may be updated at different times and with different frequency. In some cases, risk management systems are more frequently updated for market risk than for credit risk – market risk reports may be available to management intraday or even in real time, whereas credit risk reports are available daily or even less frequently.

Where data capture is automated, trade details entered at the trading desk flow automatically into risk management and trade processing systems. The risk management systems are generally updated with trade information on the trade date, providing management with timely reports.

Settlement

Depending on the product and contract terms, OTC derivatives contracts may require payments periodically throughout the life of a trade, on maturity, or combination of both. Standard settlement instructions (SSIs), which set out the agreed details of settlement arrangements, are usually exchanged by the counterparties. Some firms maintain a database of SSIs that automatically feeds into settlement systems and systems that generate settlement confirmations. Some firms confirm settlements several days in advance of the payment date.

Master agreements, including the 1992 ISDA master agreement, provide for netting of payment obligations between the parties; this allows counterparties to make a single payment in each currency. However, due to system limitations and lack of cross product integration, most payments are still made on gross basis.

Collateralization

The use of collateral to mitigate credit exposure in the OTC derivatives market has increased rapidly in recent years.

While the use of collateral mitigates credit risk, it is also considered to be a source of legal and operational risks. Additional legal agreements have to be in place, and their enforceability addressed. There also need to be additional systems and procedures to ensure that collateral is called from counterparties where needed and its receipt monitored. There needs to be monitoring of the type of collateral that is acceptable, any haircut that needs to be applied as well as rules for and frequency of revaluation.

Central clearing for OTC derivatives

There is increased interest in the use of clearing houses to centrally clear the OTC derivatives products in a similar manner to exchange-traded derivatives. The clearing house could then act as counterparty to both sides of the transaction. The use of a clearing house has the potential to mitigate some of the risks associated with OTC derivatives.

With respect to credit risk, clearing would achieve multilateral netting, which would reduce its members' credit exposures. The clearing house would be able to manage the net exposure on a daily basis through the margining arrangements. However, because clearing houses currently plan to clear only relatively simple instruments, the benefits of multilateral netting may be limited.

Legal risk would also tend to be reduced by centralized clearing. A clearing house's default procedures are often supported by specific provisions of national law, and a clearing house is highly unlikely to permit the kinds of delays in completing documentation that are observed for non-cleared transactions.

A clearing house could also reduce operational risks by imposing high standards of operational reliability on its members and by promoting further development of automated systems for confirming transactions.

However, from a systemic perspective, clearing houses tend to concentrate risks and responsibilities for risk management. The key issue is how effectively a clearing house manages the risks to which it is exposed.

Notes

1 Chance, Don, *Brief History of Derivatives*, Vol. 1, No. 34, November 1995, pp. 13–20.
2 Trading Volumes, *Futures Industry*, December 1998/January 1999, p. 5.
3 Trading Volumes, *Futures Industry*, December 1998/January 1999, p. 5.

4 Parikh S., *Electronic futures markets versus floor trading: Implications for interface design*. Paper as CHI '95, Conference on Human Factors in Computing Systems, May 1995.

5 Exchange codes are explained in Appendix 2.

6 Wahler, T.L., Plugging In The Pit, *Futures Industry*, January 1998, pp. 11–13.

7 Seat Prices, *Futures and OTC World*, November 1998, p. 71.

8 Managing Risk – The Structure and Operation of LIFFE, London International Financial Futures Exchange, 1996.

5 | Operational risk survey carried out for this book

As part of the research for this book, a series of in-depth interviews were conducted with practitioners from within the financial markets industry. The interviews focused on the current organizational structures, people, processes and technology within the operations functions. During the discussions, the interviewees were encouraged to outline their organization's policies to risk management in general and operational risk in particular.

The interviews were conducted with senior personnel within the organizations who either had responsibility for the operations area or were responsible for operational risk management. A market supervision and compliance manager from a futures and options exchange in London was interviewed to provide an exchange perspective on its own operational risk management as well as its responsibility to ensure the correct market operation through member audits and inspections. Additionally, information systems suppliers and management consultancies were interviewed.

The financial institutions selected for the research ranged from small brokers who traded only in London to large and diverse investment banks that traded in all the major financial centres. The operations varied from small administrative functions that provided support for the house traders to large multi-functional departments that were set up as profit centres to provide full clearing and settlement services for both client and house trading. The selected sample of banks included American, European and Japanese institutions.

As most of the institutions insisted on anonymity as a precondition for the interviews, it has been decided not to name any organization in this book. However, the cross section of the selected organizations provides a representative subset of the financial markets industry.

The survey was conducted through semi-structured interviews. The aim of these interviews was to discuss operational risk with people who were actively involved in managing the issues on a daily basis.

The interview format was devised to elicit the participants' views on the importance of operational risk and their direct experiences on how organizations are looking to manage this risk. All interviewees were assured that the interviews were personal and confidential and that neither their names nor the names of their organizations will be used in the subsequent publication.

The primary research concentrated on the investment banks. There are, however, many other users of financial markets and derivatives including insurance companies, fund managers, pension funds as well as corporates. Whilst these organizations were excluded from the research, it was felt that the issues raised in this study are just as applicable to them as they are to the investment banks.

Results of the market survey

Detailed contents analysis of all primary research and interview material allowed the:
1 identification of the operational risk parameters
2 development of a generic profile for the operations area including details of the organizational structure, personnel, processes and systems.

Operational risk parameters identified during the survey

Table 5.1 Operational risk parameters identified during the survey

Risk type	No of occurrences	Institutions											
		A	B	C	D	E	F	G	H	I	J	K	L
Lack of overall responsibility	3	✓			✓						✓		
Processing	12	✓	✓	✓	✓	✓	✓	✓	✓	✓	✓	✓	✓
Inexperienced staff	9	✓		✓	✓	✓	✓	✓		✓	✓	✓	✓
Inability to attract high calibre staff	4	✓				✓			✓				✓
Fraud	11	✓	✓	✓	✓	✓	✓	✓	✓	✓	✓	✓	✓
Lack of adequate systems	9	✓		✓	✓	✓		✓	✓	✓		✓	✓
Lack of system integration	4		✓	✓	✓	✓				✓		✓	✓
Inadequate controls	6		✓	✓			✓		✓			✓	
Inadequate MIS	8	✓	✓	✓	✓		✓	✓			✓	✓	✓
Inadequate monitoring	7	✓	✓	✓		✓	✓	✓		✓		✓	✓
Lack of auditors' knowledge	3	✓			✓			✓					
Country risk	3	✓							✓			✓	
Reputation risk	3	✓	✓				✓						

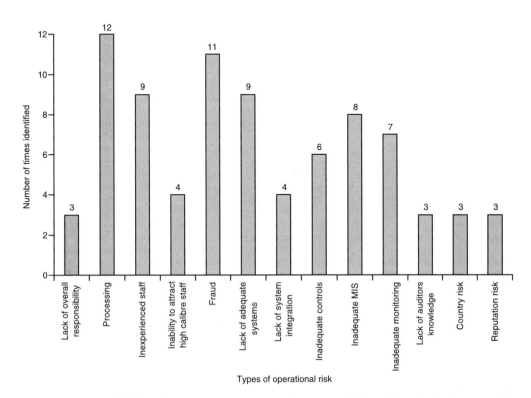

Figure 5.1 Operational risk parameters identified during the survey.

Organizational structure identified during the survey

Operations department is a general term used to denote the area that deals specifically with the administration of the various instruments traded by the institution. This includes clearing, settlement, and control of all financial products including both securities and derivatives (both exchange-traded and OTC) products. This function or department may also be referred to as 'back office' and 'dealer support'.

The primary research has allowed for the development of a generic relationship of the operations department with organiza-

Organizational structure identified during the survey

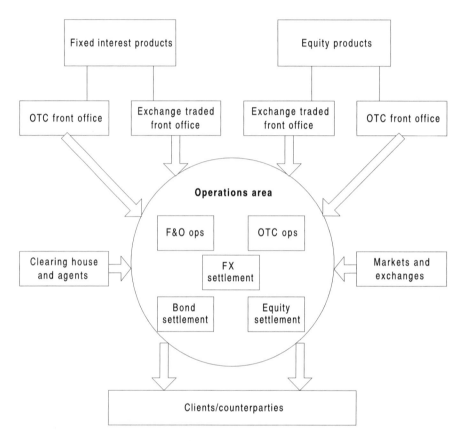

Figure 5.2 Relationships of an operations department within an organization.

tional structures as well as the organizational model for the operations department.

While there are many models for the organizational structure within investment banks, the operations function within many institutions has developed in response to the administrative and support requirements of the trading activity. Since the organization structure of most banks is based along product lines, the operations function has evolved in a similar fashion. In most organizations the administration of ETD and OTC derivatives is carried out in separate departments; in fact a few institutions still have separate administration for principal and client business. It is not unusual to see several small operations function within an organization catering for the different types of business and products, i.e. bond settlement, equity settlement, OTC settlement, and exchange traded settlement.

The survey also revealed that the trend within the industry is for closer integration of these settlement functions to provide a consolidated view of the financial and trading positions for reporting and risk management purposes. The other important development highlighted during the research is that rather than seeing the operation as merely a support function; many organizations are beginning to see it as a potential profit centre that generates revenue and adds value to the sales and marketing effort. It is no longer enough to offer the best execution service; clients are also looking for banks and brokers to demonstrate control and efficiency within their settlement and administration functions.

Operations structure

The structure of the operations function varies substantially for different organizations. It depends on the size of the organization, the type of business profile, and whether the trading is primarily for the house or clients. For example a large multinational bank that trades on many markets for the house as well as clients will have a totally different structure than a small fund manager who is using derivations to hedge his sterling based portfolio. However, the primary research has shown that there are a number of basic functions that need to be carried out regardless of the size and the content of the business.

There are four main sections that handle the workflow and the control activities in the back office. A manager from within each section reports to the director through an operations committee which meets daily to ensure that any problems are aired and

Organizational structure identified during the survey

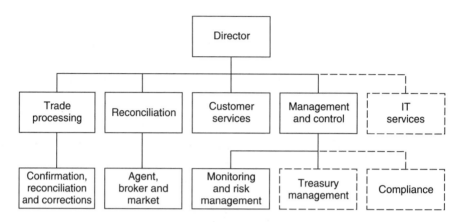

Figure 5.3 A generic structure for an operations department.

resolved. Below each of the main sections may be one or more sub-sections, which deal with specific areas or tasks that have been separated, either because of the need to segregate functions or because they require special skills. The management and control section, for example, performs a vital role within the operations area and is likely to be staffed by senior personnel. It is responsible for monitoring exposure, ensuring that correct processes and procedures are implemented, ensuring the integrity and quality of the management data and also for building relationships with agents, brokers and clients. The other important functions that are likely to be within this section are treasury management and compliance. Depending on the size of the operations area, this section may be split into a number of sub-sections responsible for individual tasks.

Underpinning the whole of the operations structure is information technology and System Support function. Technology is now such an integral and fundamental part of this business that it has an impact across all the functional areas and sections within an operation. The IT function may be part of the operations area reporting to the operations director or it may sit outside providing support from a central pool of resources. Either way, IT needs to work very closely with the business units to provide the level and quality of support necessary.

The tasks performed by the sections described above collectively cover all the clearing, settlement and administration processes. Some of these processes, such as trade confirmation and monitoring, are applicable to all product lines whilst others, such as reconciliation to the exchange or agent brokers, may only be applicable to exchange-traded derivatives processes. It is important to understand what these processes are and how they affect the running of the operations area.

Trade processing

The trade processing function within the operations area is likely to deal with all the trades, both exchange traded and OTC, that have been initiated during the day. This would involve capturing the trades, manually from faxes or deal tickets or from automatic feeds from the exchanges or other systems, ensuring the integrity of the details and carrying out any corrections and amendments that are necessary.

Open outcry trading

The largest futures exchanges in the world, i.e. Chicago Board of Trade (CBOT) and Chicago Mercantile Exchange (CME) use the open outcry method of trading. LIFFE has recently moved to list all its products on an electronic trading platform called LIFFE Connect.

To place an order under this method, the customer calls a broker, who time stamps the order and prepares an office order ticket. The broker then sends the order to the booth on the trading floor. There, a floor order ticket is prepared, and a clerk hand delivers the order to the floor trader for execution. The floor trader, standing in a central location called a trading pit, negotiates a price by shouting out the order to other floor traders, who bid on the order using hand signals. Once filled, the order is recorded in a clearing house system that matches all the trades. The clearing house ensures that there are no discrepancies in the matched trade information.

Electronic trading

An automated trade execution system has three components:

1 Computer terminals where customer orders are keyed in and trade confirmations are received.

2 An exchange host computer that processes all the trades.

3 A network that links the terminals to the host computer.

Customers may enter orders directly into the terminals or trade through a broker. The electronic order matching system then matches bids with offers according to defined rules that determine the order's priority. Priority rules on most systems include price and time of entry and in some cases include order size, type and identity of the customer. Matching occurs when a trader places a buy order at a price equal to or higher than the price of an existing sell order in the same contract. The system automatically executes the order so that the trades are matched immediately.

Reconciliation of positions

The input of trades throughout the day will result in changing positions in the accounts at the exchange/clearing house and in the internal systems.

The positions at the close of business must be reconciled because:

● The traders' dealing position must be confirmed prior to the market opening next business day. Trading on incorrect positions or outstanding unmatched trades can result in significant loss.

● Clients must have their positions confirmed prior to the market opening next business day. Incorrect registering and or reporting of positions may result in the broker having to make good substantial losses.

- The clearing house or agent will call margin on the registered open positions. Incorrect positions or assignment to wrong accounts can result in more collateral than necessary being used.

- Unreconciled positions will affect the accuracy of profit/loss reporting and input to risk management systems.

Adjusting trade errors

Unmatched and trade errors must be identified and rectified as quickly as possible if the risk of substantial loss is to be minimized. Transactions in futures and options markets, particularly open-outcry, can be prone to errors. Often these are straightforward and easily amended. Others are caused by fundamental differences and need careful and speedy rectification. Some errors and mismatches carry little risk; others have massive risk consequences.

Reconciliations

In addition to trade data and positions, there are many other important reconciliations that need to be carried out in the back office. Many of these act as a secondary level of defence against trade errors as well as detecting and preventing fraud. As brokers are required to hold separate accounts for proprietary business and client segregated business then these reconciliations are completed individually.

Table 5.2 shows the types of reconciliation that need to be performed.

Client services section

In most organizations this is a separate function which only deals with the settlement of business directly with clients. These clients could be internal clients such as other departments' trading

Table 5.2 Types of reconciliation

Clearing house or agent broker balances	A full reconciliation should take place of all balances held with the clearing house or agent broker. This includes variation margin movements.
Margin calls	The amount of margin called from the clearing house or agent broker must be equal to or less than the total amount being collected from clients.
Market close outs	Futures positions must be checked carefully to ensure that they have been correctly closed out and that the position in the internal computer system corresponds to that at the clearing house or agent broker.
Contracts exercised and assigned	These details must be carefully checked and advised to the client or traders immediately. Settlement details for the underlying asset must be checked.
Commission	A check should be made to ensure that the clearing house or agent broker has charged the correct amount of commission. The commission associated with any trades should be given-up or taken-up.
Interest	The balance of funds that is receiving, or being charged, interest must be checked as well as the rate of interest.
Collateral	The type, amount and valuation of collateral that has been deposited at the clearing house or agent broker must be reconciled against the clients' holdings.
Cash movement	In addition to reconciling the ledger balances, the individual movements must be checked. This would cover cash amounts paid and received, bank charges and payment instructions.

accounts, proprietary traders, branch offices and subsidiary companies, or external clients, which might be fund management houses, other banks or brokerage houses and private clients.

In addition to these primary functions outlined in the processing section, the client services team may be involved in the monitoring, calculation and payment of floorbrokerage to and from other brokers. They also have a crucial role in risk management as they have close contact with and knowledge of the client.

The client services team also becomes involved with marketing to clients because of the increasing importance of the back office function and operational risk. They may be required to demonstrate to potential or existing clients evidence of controls and procedures in place as well as giving advice on various operational functions. Client services receive many varied requests from their clients with regard to the settlement process which has led to the provision of what is termed added value services.

Over-the-counter settlement involves a different set of processes and skill sets. The client services team settling OTCs must be aware of the payment dates and may have to margin and value products periodically.

Management and control section

This section is likely to be staffed by senior and experienced personnel as it serves a pivotal role in maintaining a safe and successful business. The responsibility to process and provide accurate data and the ability to understand the need for and have good interaction with this section are fundamental requirements for all staff.

The management and control function has four key responsibilities:

- relationships,

- trading and positions,

- financial, and

Organizational structure identified during the survey

- reporting.

Within each of these areas the section establishes, implements and monitors procedures to ensure the effective, efficient and secure clearing, settlement and administration of the derivatives operation.

Relationships

There are numerous counterparties to the operations department and cultivating good relationships is essential to the smooth running of the operations department. Problems will inevitably occur and the quality of the relationship will determine whether the problem escalates into a crisis or is effectively and efficiently handled.

A client that is consistently late in paying money or providing collateral may just be inefficient or may be hinting at deeper problems and issues that could potentially lead to a default. Either way, the client is putting the broker at risk and an assessment of the

Figure 5.4 Various counterparties to the back office.

true situation is urgently needed. However, equally the client may be experiencing difficulties and be trying to rectify the situation. If the broker approaches the client too aggressively or insensitively the client may well feel embarrassed and the result could be a termination of the relationship. The fine balance between firmness or help and risk management is extremely important.

Trading, ledgers and positions

The operations department has a key role to play in ensuring a safe and efficient business. It is critical to establishment controls to ensure that the correct procedures and processes are being performed, that they are effective, and any issues highlighted are addressed and remedial actions taken quickly and effectively.

Controls will include the effective segregation of functions, random reconciliation checks, rotating of staff where necessary and analysis of information from the various processing and reconciliation functions.

Financial

With derivatives being settled on trade day +1 and with margin calls on positions that may change daily, coupled with interest payments and cash receipts and payments, managing the financial aspects of the derivatives operations area is a complex and continuous process.

Control over the quality of the financial information being generated is critically important. In the UK for instance, a broker cannot use one client's money or assets to offset a shortfall in another client's account. The liability must be met by the broker and made good by him depositing his own money or assets to the value of the short fall into his designated client account at the bank or clearing organization. The information on margin requirements and settlement to clients is needed as soon as possible and the team needs to ensure that the clients settle their liabilities in a timely manner. If this is not done then the broker may end up incurring substantial funding costs as well as potentially being at risk to default.

Reporting

There are numerous demands on the operations department for reporting. This may emanate from internal or external sources. Key reporting requirements include:

- risk management,

- regulatory, and

- management information.

As with the information on financial matters, the quality, relevance and timeliness of information is essential.

1997 Operational Risk Management Survey

British Bankers Association (BBA) in conjunction with Coopers & Lybrand conducted a survey[1] in 1997 to quantify the concern that banks have regarding operational risk. Forty-five of BBA's members, covering a broad spectrum of the banking industry in the UK, participated in the survey. The business areas covered by the survey included retail banking, global custody, fund management as well as treasury and capital markets.

The significant finds of the survey included:

- More than 67% of the banks thought that operational risk was as significant or more significant then either market or credit risk.

- 24% of the banks had experienced individual losses of more than £1m in the last three years.

- 47% identified treasury and capital markets as the business area most likely to suffer loss.

- Reported types of losses are shown in Figure 5.5.

- 33% of the banks did not evaluate the impact of operational risk.

- 62% of the banks expect to make changes to their approach to operational risk in the next two years.

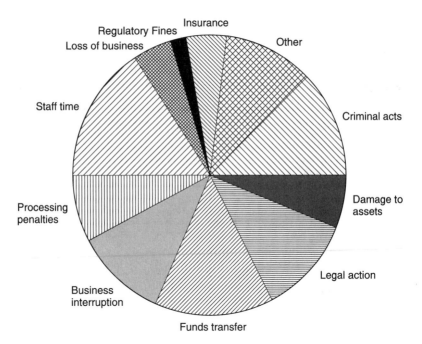

Figure 5.5 Types of losses.

Operations cultural model

During the research for this book, it has been possible to construct a generic cultural model for an operations department. The institutions visited during the course of the research varied in terms of size, nationality and organizational structures. The attitude to operational risk management varied substantially; the type and profile of the back office personnel was also quite varied. However, there were sufficient similarities between the various operations to generate a generic cultural model. The cultural model that best fits the operations departments is a bureaucratic culture where:

- Work is co-ordinated from the top.

- Power is through position in the organization.

- Rules and procedures are the major methods of influence.

- Performance above the role is not usually required.

The cultural web, i.e. symbols, stories and myths, rituals and routines, control systems, organizational structure and power structure, of these organizations constantly reinforces this paradigm within the operations areas. Although this provides security and stability in a stable environment, it has also meant that:

- There is relatively little innovation.

- The use of technology is primarily to automate some of the manual tasks rather than re-engineer the processes.

- The operations functions within banks have not perceived the need for change and have been slow to react to the changing market place.

- The role of the individuals within the department has changed very little over the last decade.

Bureaucratic cultures such as this are unable to cope with rapid and unpredictable change, increasing complexity of the business and the diversity of specialist expertise. This is substantially borne out in the case of operations within investment institutions. While there have been some improvements within the operations function facilitated primarily by introduction of technology, there have been no substantial changes or innovations in the role or the scope of the back office. This is due to the fact that the whole financial industry has a fixed mindset for the role of the operations area, i.e. that of providing clerical support to the trading function. While this approach worked well before the current information age, this paradigm paralysis or fixed mindset has resulted in organizations trying to cope with new challenges through use of inappropriate models and tools. The problem with mindsets or paradigms is that they tend to filter our perception of the world and the initiatives and advances outside the paradigm are neglected and overlooked.

The operations paradigm is that:

- It provides administration support to the front office.

- It is a cost centre rather than profit centre.

- It is staffed by young and inexperienced people. The staff are not of the highest calibre.

- It adds very little value to the company or its products.

- It does not have a substantial role to play in risk management.

This fixed mindset has resulted in organizations failing to take advantage of the opportunities offered by the combination of the central role of the back office and the advances in technology, particularly in the areas of communication and data management.

Note

1 British Bankers Association and Coopers & Lybrand, *1997 Operational Risk Management Survey*, May 1997.

6 | Risk spectrum

In the late 1980s and early 1990s, few people within the financial markets discussed risk or risk management. Banks and financial institutions, who were generally considered to be well managed and relatively low risk institutions, were monitored on the their liquidity ratios. The regulators were primarily worried about the credit risk of the off-balance-sheet products like derivatives and therefore instigated capital adequacy requirement framework in the late 1980s and subsequently introduced proposals for monitoring market risk in the early 1990s. The generating departments monitored their own risk within the banks.

However, risk is now *the* paramount topic within the financial sector. The emphasis has switched from making money to not losing it. Previous chapters in this book have outlined some of the recent problems that have necessitated a greater focus on risk management. These problems include:

- $1.06 billion losses at CSFB;

- $3.5 billion rescue package of the Long-Term Capital Management fund;

- the collapse of Barings;

- concealment at Diawa and Sumitomo;

- $1.8 billion losses at Metallgesellschaft AG.

No unique risks to users of derivatives

While the increased use of derivatives is new, derivatives are composed of financial instruments and arrangements that have been around for decades. It is therefore not surprising that the risks to users of derivatives, i.e. credit, market and operational, are neither new nor unique. They are the same types of risks that banks and financial institutions face in their traditional businesses and which are endemic to 'traditional' balance sheet financial contracts such as mortgage loans, commercial paper, certificates of deposits, and the financing of securities positions.

Credit risk to both parties in a derivatives transaction is the risk that a loss will be incurred because the party fails to make the payments due. In the event of default, the loss is the cost of replacing the derivatives contract with a new party. Some derivatives transactions also exhibit a type of credit risk known as settlement and payments risk. Same-day settlement risk exists when delivery of an asset or security is not synchronized with the receipt of payment; the security can be surrendered and payment never received. The same risk exists when gross payments are exchanged, rather than a single 'netted' payment. Netting is the process by which multiple gross payments are netted into single cash flows.

Market risk is the risk that the value of a contract, financial instrument, asset, or portfolio will change when market conditions change. Interest rate risk is a common form of market risk. For example, if the duration mismatch between the assets and liabilities of a bank exposes it to losses due to interest rate changes, that institution bears market risk akin to the risk borne by a holder of a corporate bond. A fixed-for-floating interest rate swap likewise has the same market risk as a fixed-rate loan funded with floating-rate deposits. Like credit risk, market risk must be viewed from a portfolio or balance sheet perspective. A bank's exposure to interest rate risk, for example, is determined by the combination of the bank's interest-rate-sensitive balance sheet items with its off-balance sheet, interest-rate-sensitive items, including derivatives.

All users of financial products face operational risk, or the risk that losses will be incurred as a result of inadequate systems and internal controls, inadequate disaster or contingency planning, human error, or management failure. Entering into complex derivatives positions without adequate systems for measuring, monitoring, and controlling market or credit risk is an example of operational risk. An aspect of operational risk that has received significant attention recently is the risk management or internal control and oversight process. A failure at any point in the risk management chain constitutes operational risk and can result in significant losses.

The total spectrum of risks[1] is shown in Figure 6.1; it includes both global risks and organizational risks.

Risk categories

There are three main categories of risk that an organization experiences when operating in financial markets. These categories are market risk, credit risk and operational risk.

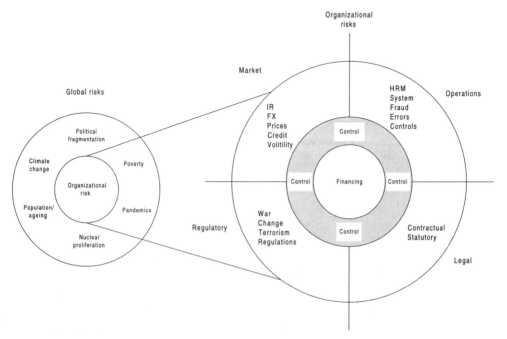

Figure 6.1 The total spectrum of risks.

Market risk

Market risk is the risk to a bank's financial condition resulting from adverse movements in market prices. Accurately measuring an institution's market risk requires timely information about the current market values of its assets, liabilities, and off-balance-sheet positions. Market risk arises from factors such as changing interest rates and currency exchange rates, the liquidity of markets for specific commodities or financial instruments, and local or world political and economic events. All of these sources of potential market risk can affect the value of the institution and should be considered in the risk measurement process.

Market risk is the risk due to the movements in the market having an adverse effect of your portfolio. It includes

Price risk

- Changes in market prices.

- Changes in market volatility.

- Lack of market liquidity.

Interest rate risk

- Changes in interest rates.

- Changes in interest rate volatility.

- Changes in the shape of the yield curve.

Currency risk

- Changes in exchange rates.

- Changes in exchange rate volatility.

- Changes to the value of profit raised abroad on conversion to base currency.

Credit risk

Broadly defined, credit risk is the risk that a counterparty will fail to perform on an obligation to the financial institution. It involves both settlement and pre-settlement credit risk for customers across all products. On settlement day, the exposure to counterparty default may equal the full value of any cash flows or securities the institution is to receive. Prior to settlement, credit risk is measured as the sum of the replacement cost of the position, plus an estimate of the bank's potential future exposure from the instrument as a result of market changes. Credit risk includes:

- *Direct credit risk* – Counterparty default on on-balance-sheet products, e.g. loans or issued debts, where the exposure is full face value.

- *Credit equivalent exposure* – Counterparty default on unmatured off-balance-sheet products, e.g. swaps or options, where the 'credit equivalent exposure' is the function of the current market prices.

- *Settlement risk* – Counterparty default on transactions in the process of being settled and where the value has been delivered to the counterparty but not yet received in return.

Operational risk

Operational risk is by far the most extensive risk category. At its broadest, it is defined as everything that is not market and credit. It can range from a natural disaster, which can cause the loss of a primary trading site, to a difference in the payment conventions on a foreign exchange transaction. It includes such matters as inappropriate organizational structure, inadequate systems, failure to properly supervise, defective controls, fraud, legal and regulatory issues and human error. The difference between operational risk and operations risk also becomes apparent when defining the total constituent categories of operational risk. Operational risk includes:

- portfolio risk;

- organizational risk;

- strategic risk, personnel risk;

- change management risk;

- operations risk;

- currency risk

- country risk

- shift in credit rating;

- reputation risk;

- taxation risk;

- legal risk;

- business continuity risk; and

- regulatory or compliance risk.

Portfolio risk

This is the risk due to the concentration of exposure in a specific instrument, in a single transaction or within an industry sector or country. A recent example of problems rising from concentration of financial exposure in a country was the substantial losses incurred by many institutions in Russia.

Organizational risk

This is the risk of inadequate or inappropriate organizational structure, people or processes in place for the type of business being transacted. Inappropriate organizational structure can lead to misunderstandings or lack of clarity over who has responsibility for particular areas or issues. The main problem with organizational risk is that it can remain undetected and put the institution at great risk. An ineffective organizational structure can lead to lapses in internal controls and a weak decision making process. Whilst the problems created by weak structures and unclear reporting line are well documented, strong and rigid organizational structure can also expose the institution to risk. Organizational risk includes:

- blurred lines of communications

- weak or ill-defined responsibility matrix

- lack of expertise within the management team to adequately control the business;

- lack of expertise about the products being traded;

- inadequate or incomplete management information systems;

- lack of segregation between front and back office;

- poor management supervision.

Strategic risk

Strategic risk is the risk to earnings or capital arising from adverse business decisions or improper implementation of those decisions. This risk is a function of the incompatibility of an organization's strategic goals, the business strategies developed to achieve those goals, the resources deployed against these goals, and the quality of implementation processes. The resources needed to carry out business strategies are both tangible and intangible. They include communication channels, operating systems, delivery networks, and managerial capacities and capabilities.

Personnel risk

Personnel risk can occur both within the operations area as well as within the organization generally. It is the risk of not having sufficiently qualified or experienced people within the organization to adequately manage and control the level or type of business. Personnel are the key resource for any organization; this is particularly the case for a financial institution.

The calibre of the management is also fundamental to the success of the organization. This is particularly so in the current climate of consolidation and change within the financial industry.

In the trading environment within financial markets the ability to receive, assimilate and react quickly and efficiently to continuously changing situations is fundamental to an institution's operation. As well as the technological infrastructure, this requires skilled and experienced personnel to be available in the organization. The greater emphasis on risk management within financial institutions requires skilled staff to measure, monitor and control risk.

In order to take advantage of developments and to create innovative technological solutions, financial institutions need to ensure that they have the required staff, skills and development programmes. Management needs to ensure that they can recruit, retain and develop their staff and to ensure that they manage the employee relationships effectively in order to fully tap their skills and commitment.

The personnel within the operations area are generally categorized as young and of limited experience both in terms of technology and business. In a fast moving and complex market this can be a big liability.

Change management risk

The drive for globalization, technological and organizational developments are producing substantial change within the financial industry and the pace of change is accelerating. Effective management of change, therefore, has become a key management activity and is central to the success of an organization. The risk due to the failure of change management programmes or their effective integration into the business is very real in the current climate. The challenge for organizations is to effectively manage the transition, deal with organizational cultures and handle organizational politics.

Operations risk

A key constituent of operational risk is operations risk. These two types of risks are frequently confused. Operations risk specifically refers to the risks encountered in the back office. It includes transactions processing, reconciliation, controls and procedures, personnel and systems and technology employed in the operations area.

Processing risk

Processing risk includes all the issues associated with trade captures, reconciliation and trade and settlement processing. With greater use of technology, office automation and straight through processing, this type of risk can be substantially reduced. The majority of the 'operational risk management systems' that are currently available primarily address this type of processing risk. Processing and transactional risk include:

- errors in processing of transactions;

- errors in execution of trades;

- errors arising from complexity of products and inability of existing systems and procedures to cater for them;

- errors in booking trades;

- errors in the settlement of trades;

- errors in delivery processes; and

- inadequate legal documentation.

Operations procedures and control risk

> This results from inappropriate or unusable procedures and inadequate controls for monitoring the business. During the primary research interviews, it became apparent that many institutions had detailed operational and procedures manuals but many were rarely used because they were either out of date or bore little relation to how the jobs were currently carried out. Operational procedures and control risks include:
>
> - breakdown of controls and procedures around the front and back offices;
>
> - unidentified breach of trading limits;
>
> - unauthorized trading by individual traders;
>
> - fraudulent practices related to trading or processing activities, including false accounting and forgery;
>
> - money laundering;
>
> - unauthorized access to systems or models;
>
> - dependency on a limited number of key people; and
>
> - lack of controls around the processing of trades.

Technology and systems risk

> Technology and systems are central to the financial institutions. Technology plays a key role in the operations area as well as across the organization. A lot of the processing and evaluations cannot be carried out without the use of complex mathematical models and computer systems.
>
> Technology has become such a central component within the banking environment that any systems or communication problems can have a catastrophic impact on an institution. Technology risk occurs where there are no adequate plans for managing and monitoring the performance of technology related to projects,

products or services. Technology risk can occur where the organization invests in the latest, and often untried, technology as well as where there is little or no investment in advanced technology. Additionally the reliance of many banks and financial institutions on third party software products and on external organizations for managing their data centres adds supplier risk to the equation. Technology risk also includes information system project management risk. This includes:

- *Technology risk* – The use of new and untried technology can have a detrimental impact on the business. There is the potential that technology may not be able to meet the required needs of the business. Additionally, the infrastructure and the workforce may not be able to cope with the new technology.

- *Scheduling risk* – This is the risk of delays or non-delivery of a project due to inadequate task estimation, status reporting or progress monitoring.

- *Financial risk* – This is the risk of exhaustion of funds before the completion of the project. Management of the costs for a project may be compromised due to inadequate budgeting, financial reporting or financial control.

- *External risk* – The external factors include reliance on third parties for development, testing or implementation services. Delivery risk is increased where there are multiple vendors or where the solution involves integrating components from a number of different suppliers. This is due to the difficulty of enforcing consistent standards during testing and change control.

- *Implementation risk* – This occurs due to lack of skilled resources, inadequate procedures or tools for the business activity. One of the recurring problems during implementation is the under-estimation of converting data from the old system to the new system.

Additional issues for technology and system risk include:

- Errors in the development of software. The complex nature of the investment banking industry means that any support system would require complex algorithms or business rules to be developed. Unless there is comprehensive testing, there is a risk that the algorithms may be incorrectly programmed.

- Errors in the formulae or mathematical models. The nature of derivatives products require development of complex models for revaluation purposes. As new products are developed, these models need to be continually updated.

- Errors or failures in system support.

- Errors in calculating mark to market amounts.

- Inadequate or untimely management of information.

- Failure in key systems required to support business activities.

- Failure in network or communication channels.

- Inappropriate release or misuse of information.

- Inability of suppliers to deliver on time and within budget.

- Inadequate functionality.

- Inadequate or non-existent contingency planning in the case of system or communications failure.

Information risk

While the need for strong internal controls surrounding information systems has always been recognized, technological developments over the last few years have increased many of the business control risks and have exposed information systems to new risks through:

- The increase in end-user computing through the use of user-driven development tools and client-server architectures has made it more difficult to manage and control systems and data. While end-user developments reduce the ever increasing burden on the organization's IT staff and provide many advantages, they also make it very difficult to monitor and control security standards.

- The development in telecommunications has allowed organizations to develop closer links by increased sharing of information both nationally and internationally. There is increased automation of financial transactions between organizations. The development in e-commerce is set to increase the volume of electronic financial transactions.

- The increased outsourcing of various aspects of information systems to third parties can potentially reduce the effectiveness of internal organizational controls.

- Effective use of technology allows organizations to gain increased operational efficiency as well as competitive or strategic advantage. This, allied with the improved performance of computer equipment and their significantly reduced cost, has meant that there is greater reliance on technology and computers in financial organizations.

The net effect of these trends is that most organizations are susceptible to:

- Manipulation of data to defraud the organization, either for gain or for management purposes.

- Intentional or unintentional disclosure of sensitive data.

- Destruction of valuable assets (e.g., applications or data), causing a disruption of vital services.

- Information and data is one of the most significant assets of a financial institution. Market data and information from in-house systems forms the basis of many trading and risk management decisions. When data and information is inaccessible, corrupted, incorrect or lost, it can expose the institution to a substantial risk.

Thus, it is essential that organizations ensure that all their IT infrastructure and systems contain the necessary security provisions to reduce these potential risks through the implementation of effective security and control measures. This is particularly important as organizations begin to develop data warehouses and knowledge management systems.

Currency risk

Currency risk occurs due to exposure in a foreign currency. This risk includes:

- *Convertibility risk* – This the inability to convert one currency into another as a result of political/economic policy (i.e. exchange rate controls, devaluation etc.).

- *Translation risk* – This is the profit/loss due to translation of financial statements of an overseas subsidiary into the home currency for consolidation.

- *Transaction risk* – This is risk of movements in the foreign exchange rates when credit transactions are denominated in a foreign currency.

- *Economic risk* – This arises when the present value of future cashflows changes due to a change in the exchange rates.

Country risk

Country risk is the risks faced by institutions undertaking business in various countries around the globe. It includes components such as political, financial and economic risks as well as risks related to the general business concerns of stability and social turmoil. Many institutions have suffered substantial losses due to financial, political and social instabilities in many Far Eastern former 'tiger economies'. The collapse of the financial infrastructure in Russia has resulted in severe losses for many western financial institutions that had exposure in that country.

Shift in credit rating

Inability to raise funds at acceptable cost or access markets due to adverse movement in credit ratings. During the currency crisis of 1998, many Japanese banks had suffered from downgraded credit ratings, making them less attractive to counterparties wanting A or AA credit ratings.

Reputation risk

Reputation risk is the risk to earnings or capital arising from negative public opinion. This affects the institution's ability to establish new relationships or services, or to continue servicing existing relationships. This risk can expose the institution to litigation, financial loss, or damage to its reputation. Reputation risk exposure is present throughout the organization and is why banks always exercise caution in dealing with their customers and the community.

Technology has made it possible for financial institutions to deal directly with customers on a real time basis through many different channels. However, this has also made it easier for customers to move from one institution to another. Additionally, branding of financial services and products is becoming more important. As financial institutions begin to engage in a vast range of new business in competitive markets, positive name recognition becomes an indispensable asset. Reputation risk is different from some of the other types of risk in that it normally arises when other controls have failed. It is, therefore, a symptom of other risks rather than a cause. However, it can have a serious impact on the institutions' brand name and can take a long time to redress.

Taxation risk

Changes in tax laws or unanticipated tax laws.

Legal risk

Breach of legal requirements in the effective jurisdiction. The developments in technology and increased globalization mean an institution has access to many more markets in more countries, resulting in more complex legal issues. This is further complicated with the expansion of products and the development of new delivery channels.

Business continuity risk

Business continuity risk (BCR) is caused by unforeseen events occurring that may affect an institution's ability to manage its activities. Traditionally BCR has focused on events such as natural disasters, sabotage, industrial action and wars. Therefore efforts to mitigate the effects of these events have concentrated on system and infrastructure facilities at different sites. However, any assessment of BCR must include the impact of withdrawal of IT and telecommunication systems as well as loss of key individuals or teams from the organization or collapse or suspension of financial markets.

Regulatory or compliance risk

Regulatory or compliance risk is the risk to earnings or capital arising from violations of, or non-conformance with, laws, rules, regulations, prescribed practices, or ethical standards. This risk also arises in situations where the laws or rules governing certain products or activities may be ambiguous or untested. Compliance risk exposes the institution to fines, civil money penalties, payment of damages, and the voiding of contracts. Regulatory and compliance risk can lead to a diminished reputation, reduced franchise value, limited business opportunities, lessened expansion potential, and the lack of contract enforceability. It also includes:

- inability to meet regulatory requirements;

- breaching existing capital requirements;

- failure to anticipate forthcoming regulatory requirements.

Note

1 Kloman H H, *Rethinking Risk Management*, Geneva Papers, July 1992.

7 | **Managing operational risk**

Introduction

The collapse of Barings, Britain's oldest merchant bank, and the
$1.8 billion losses suffered by Sumitomo Corporation catapulted
the need for managing operational risk into corporate conscious-
ness. Sound operational risk management is essential to the
prudent operation of a financial institution and to promoting stability in the financial system as a whole. While risk management
is often defined as hedging or neutralizing the financial risks that
result from a series of transactions, operational risk is defined as
the entire process of policies, procedures, expertise and systems
that an institution needs in order to manage all the risks resulting
from its financial transactions.

Operational risks can range from a natural disaster, which can
cause the loss of a primary trading site, to a difference in the
payment conventions on a foreign exchange transaction. It
includes such matters as inappropriate organizational structure,
inadequate systems, failure to properly supervise the business,
defective controls, fraud, and human error. Risk management has
become a major issue for financial institutions as technological
advances have compressed the time frame for dealing, thereby
necessitating timely risk reporting. Recent market occurrences
have also created a particularly strong sentiment for the establishment of strong risk management. Modification of operational procedures and controls are necessary, as risk management becomes
more challenging in a fast paced market. Failure to adequately
manage operational risk can negatively impact profit/loss, not
only resulting from the costs of incorrect settlement of transactions, but also managing incorrect positions or taking unknown

credit risks. Further, failure to manage operational risk can also harm a firm's reputation and cause a loss of business.

One of the key risk management practices is the segregation of duties between operations personnel and trading personnel. Operations personnel, who are responsible for confirmation and settlement, must maintain a reporting line independent of trading, where the trade execution takes place. The financial industry has been recently reminded of this very essential control, first with Barings and again with Daiwa Bank. Barings and Daiwa have alerted all organizations to focus intensely on trader and market practices as well as on operational control. These crises have prompted all levels of management to re-examine in their own organizations what they are doing and what they should be doing to minimize risk.

Operational controls are vital to the risk management process. In particular, effective controls help banks detect and resolve problems before they lead to financial loss. Many institutions have responded to this risk management dilemma by implementing tighter controls within the operations function. However, managing operational risk encompasses the co-ordinated management of business processes, human capital and technology.

Traditionally, the concept of risk for financial markets has focused on financial risks and derivatives products developed to manage them. Managing financial risks such as market and credit risk has evolved into a sophisticated science. By its nature, financial risk can be measured, monitored, and analysed. And yet, the root causes of most losses incurred by investment institutions are operational breakdowns and control weaknesses, not the mismanagement of financial risks.

Despite this fact, the industry has generally allocated few resources and limited attention to the active management of operational risk. All businesses, regardless of the activity, take on risk and the successful organizations view risk pro-actively. Risk arises both from failing to capture opportunities whilst pursuing business objectives and from a threat that something bad will happen. Within the financial markets, risk management too often focuses on the market and credit risk and has come to be regarded as the province of the select few 'rocket scientists' or risk and audit committees. This had led to organizations trying to impose controls and procedures that are either not understood by the majority of the staff or are irrelevant to the way the tasks are performed on a daily basis. This issue was highlighted many times during the research where companies had engaged either internal or external consultants to produce operations or procedures manuals for their staff. These manuals were rarely used in operations departments because they:

- were out of date almost as soon as they were produced because of the fast nature of the financial markets;

- did not reflect how the task was performed in practice;

- were rarely used since the staff had very little input into this process.

What is needed is a change of approach by the organizations; the function of management needs to change from control to tapping into the capabilities and commitment of its staff. A new integrated approach to risk management needs to be developed that involves staff and the processes at all levels of the organization. The management and the workforce need to challenge the old paradigm and develop a more flexible approach to deal with the ever more complex and changing environments. This requires the re-evaluation of the structure of the organizations, the strategy for risk management, as well as the use of information technology and the communication infrastructure.

A fully integrated approach to risk management involves determining the company's risk appetite and setting the risk management agenda. This then needs to be supported by a more holistic approach to monitoring and management that must be comprehensive, inclusive and pro-active. A comprehensive approach to risk management covers three key aspects of business organization – its strategy, its processes and its people. It must also be inclusive (involving all levels of the organization), pro-active (aiming to anticipate risks in advance) and must address all the risks identified in Chapter 6, Risk spectrum.

At a strategic level, the board must play a leading role in setting a clear risk framework. It must define the risk appetite of business and outline which risks the business will accept, and which it will it seek to transfer or modify by negotiation, insurance or a change of approach. Once the strategic framework is set, there has to be full integration into company processes. The day-to-day activities of the of the business need to support the overall risk management vision and there needs to be clear ownership and authority for risk decisions.

Risk management needs to be embedded in organizational culture and behaviour. Business managers need to understand the framework and processes of risk management and the staff must be trained in its philosophy and approach. Reward systems within the organization should be designed to encourage risk awareness and to reward behaviours that are consistent with business objectives. It is essential to involve people in all areas of the business, for staff are not only responsible for managing risks, but also contribute to the business's risk exposure through their actions. This interplay between strategic and operational considerations and the resulting involvement of all parts of the business is fundamental to this integrated approach to risk management.

By adopting this integrated risk management approach companies can identify opportunities to improve the profitability of the business, either by removing the cost of existing control tasks, or by taking on more risk where appropriate. Conversely, failure to involve all parts of the organization can lead to a fragmented or

contradictory approach in which the business may face unnecessary risks, or underestimate the potential rewards available from
accepting a specific risk.

Why manage operational risk?

Most financial institutions have taken some measures to
address operational risks. However, they generally take such
actions reactively to remedy a specific issue that has already
surfaced. Very few companies have adopted integrated, proactive
programmes for managing operational risk. The following
are a few reasons why a more integrated approach should be
adopted.

Recurring operating losses

There are recurring cases of investment institutions suffering
operating losses – losses that stem from the mismanagement of
operational risks. The specific causes of these losses vary from
year to year and from company to company, but the negative
short-term and long-term financial consequences are often significant and damaging to the business reputation.

Growing complexity of the trading environment

The increased complexity of the business – the growing sophisti-
cation of financial instruments, investment products, global
markets, and clients – requires a comparable evolution in risk
management techniques and tools. While the market will continue
to evolve and develop mitigating controls, management should
consider the following issues raised by the developments of technology, instruments and markets.

● With continued advance in technology, traders are able to
   execute many more transactions during periods of market

volatility. Greater levels of automation and straight-through processing means that there are increasing levels of data that need to be processed and managed. The banks are increasingly automating their operations both in terms of trading and customer information. The Internet is set to have a tremendous impact in the banking industry. It is increasingly becoming possible for the clients to be able to trade and transfer funds electronically. Furthermore there is a growing trend towards virtual banks and organizations. The growth in the speed and volume of information flows requires much more efficient and effective controls.

- With the technology move to client-server-based solutions, operations need to ensure that this new environment has adequate level of reliability, control, security, and recoverability.

- Volumes will continue to grow as many of the emerging nations become more active in the international capital markets.

- There is ever-increasing pressure for globalization, both of customer and products. Investment banks and their clients are increasingly looking to take advantage of global markets in order to maximize returns of their investments. Banks need to be able to react to their clients by providing global infrastructures, services and products that meet their requirements.

- The continuous development of new and more exotic types of derivatives products.

- New types of clients will continue to deal in the market. Recently, the increased activity of fund managers and investment advisors has led to the need for new trading and settlement procedures.

- Organizational structures are becoming much flatter as a result of organization development and increased use of technology.

Many institutions are going through organizational changes and restructuring in order to become more flexible, productive and profitable. Whole layers of management have been removed from organizational structures as organizations develop integrated information systems to process and disseminate information more quickly and efficiently through the organization.

- Organizations are moving more and more toward a matrix management approach that may contain more 'ambiguous lines of authority'. However, the roles and responsibilities of each area has should be clearly defined, especially for people in the operations who play an important role in the overall control environment.

- As the national economies become interlinked, organizations are also becoming global in outlook. They are becoming more decentralizsed and federal in order to take advantage of the economies of scale of a large organization while retaining a fast, more focused and flexible approach of a small organization. However, this trend toward larger regional trading hubs supporting a network of smaller satellite offices makes it much more difficult at the satellite sites to maintain proper separation of duties between trading and operations.

Client demand

The financial institutions are becoming much more customer focused. It is no longer enough for banks to offer standard services and products. Banks need to tailor their services and products to meet their client's requirements. Organizations need to 'think global and act local'. Increasingly clients and counterparties are looking for (and demanding) assurance that both adequate management structures and skilled staff are in place to minimize operational risk.

Need for integrated risk management

Without effective management of operational risk, an organization cannot monitor its market or credit risk exposure. In order to effectively manage market and credit risks, it is necessary to have the relevant skills and expertise in the staff, technical and organizational infrastructure, as well as control systems. As all of these are components of operational risk, it then becomes apparent that an integrated risk management approach needs to focus on operational risk.

Measuring operational risk

There has been a lot of work done in defining operational risk and ways of managing it. While techniques for measuring market and credit risk are well established and understood, the development of financial measures for operational risk are still at early stages. Because of its complex nature, operational risk does not easily lend itself to financial quantification. The industry has not developed any standard measurement techniques. The regulatory and supervisory community is actively thinking about capital charge for operational risk based on yet-to-be-defined standard measures of an institution's exposure to this type of risk.

The nature of operational risk makes quantitative assessment very difficult and providing financial estimates of its exposure requires a complex combination of people, processes, technology and other internal and external events. Whether a standard methodology can be developed for measuring such a disparate array of influences and events will remain the subject of passionate debate for the foreseeable future. However, institutions have begun to attempt various techniques for measuring operational risk exposure. These techniques include fixed or proportional charge based on operational costs, using statistical models based on historic information about losses and loss events and process models where each core process is analysed to determine the potential cause of each loss event.

Whatever measurement methodology organizations develop, effective management of operational risk requires an integrated approach to the development of staff skills and training, optimization of the business processes, development of a risk aware culture and a technological infrastructure that allows the organization to process, monitor and manage the business.

G-30 and Basle Committee reports on risk management

While there have been numerous reports over the past few years on the issue of risk management and control, two have made a substantial contribution to the risk management process. These two reports are:

1 Derivatives: Practices and Principles, G-30 report published in July 1993.

2 Risk Management Guidelines for Derivatives, written jointly by the Basle Committee on Banking Supervision and the International Organization of Securities Commissions (IOSCO) 1994.

These two reports together have shaped today's best practices in risk control. Both reports laid some fundamental rules for effective operational risk management. These include:

- The importance of defining the scope and policy of the firm's involvement in and use of the various financial instruments at the highest level of the organization.

- The oversight responsibility by boards of directors and senior managers within the institution.

- The need for a risk management process that involves continuous measuring, monitoring and controlling of all risks.

- The need for accurate and reliable management information with comprehensive limits.

- The need for frequent and comprehensive management reporting.

- The requirement for sound control and operational systems.

- The need for thorough audit and control procedures.

To effectively managing risk is to ensure that all the professionals involved, including trader operations and settlements staff and those responsible for supervision, have the necessary skills and experience. The institution must ensure that it does not deal in any instrument until senior managers are fully satisfied that all relevant personnel understand and can manage the risks involved.

The G-30 report addresses the issues for both dealers (financial institutions) and end-users (corporates) of derivatives. The guidelines are embodied in 20 recommendations which firms can use to set up and evaluate their risk management and control practices. The guidelines are divided into five main areas:

- general policies for senior management;

- valuation and market risk management;

- credit risk measurement and management;

- systems, operations and controls;

- recommendations for legislators, regulators, and supervisors.

The Basle Committee/IOSCO report is directed primarily towards banking organizations. It provides a framework which the institutions can follow and against which they can reassess their own risk management procedures. These guidelines include risk management practices for each major risk identified – credit, market, liquidity, operations and legal. The Basle Committee/IOSCO suggested that the entire process of measuring, monitoring and controlling risk should be consistent with the firm's established policies and it should be independent of both the trading and administration functions. This independence should be reflected in the organizational hierarchy of the institution as well as the firm's exposure-reporting system. The 1994 document has become the definitive word on best practices in risk control for derivatives.

The Basle Committee's increasing focus on sound internal controls has resulted in the publication of the Framework for the Evaluation of Internal Control Systems(1998) report. The Committee notes,

> An analysis of the problems related to the losses [incurred by several banking organizations] indicates that they could probably have been avoided had the banks maintained effective internal control systems. Such systems would have prevented or enabled earlier detection of the problems that led to the losses, thereby limiting damage to the banking organization.

The Committee noted that the control breakdowns typically seen in recent problem bank situations could be grouped into five broad categories:

1 Lack of adequate management oversight and accountability, and failure to develop a strong control culture within the bank.

2 Inadequate assessment of the risk of certain banking activities, whether on- or off-balance sheet.

3 The absence or failure of key control activities, such as segregation of duties, approvals, verifications, reconciliations, and reviews of operating performance.

4 Inadequate communication of information between levels of management within the bank, especially in the upward communication of problems.

5 Inadequate or ineffective audit programs and other monitoring services.

It is thus not surprising that the 13 principles issued by the Basle Committee cover management oversight and the control culture; risk assessment; control activities; information and communication; monitoring; and evaluation of internal control systems by supervisory authorities. The guidelines stress the important role that management has to play in developing an appropriate organizational structure, establishing robust internal controls and aligning rewards systems to commitment to risk management principles. The importance of these issues is addressed in the following principles:

- Senior management must set out and monitor the adequate and effective internal control system. They should also develop processes that identify, measure, monitor and control risks incurred by the bank. They must maintain an organizational structure that clearly assigns responsibility, authority and reporting relationships and ensure that these delegated responsibilities are effectively carried out.

- It is the role of senior management to promote a culture that is conducive to an effective system of internal control. The Committee believes that it is the responsibility of the board of directors and senior management to push home the importance of internal controls through their actions and words. For example, senior management may weaken the control culture by promoting and rewarding managers who are successful in generating profits but fail to implement internal control policies or address problems identified by internal audit. Such actions send a message to others in the organization that internal control is considered secondary to other goals in the organizations, and thus diminish the commitment to and quality of the control culture.

The Basle Committee on Banking Supervision published the report Operational Risk Management in September 1998. This outlines the results of a survey carried out by a working group committee. The report is reproduced in Appendix 2.

Risk management framework

The lapses in risk management and risk controls have led to substantial financial losses by organizations through out the 1990s. The 1997 Operational Risk Management Survey conducted by British Bankers Association (BBA) in conjunction with Coopers & Lybrand revealed that 24 per cent of the banks surveyed had experienced individual losses of more than £1m in the last three years. Barings, Morgan Grenfell Asset Management, Daiwa, Sumitomo Corporation and many other organizations suffered huge losses as a result of failures in their control systems. Therefore any comprehensive risk management framework needs to address all the risk and control issues outlined in Chapter 6, Risk spectrum. This includes market, credit and operational risks. In order to effectively manage market and credit risks it is necessary to have the relevant skills and expertise in the staff, technical and organizational infrastructure, as well as control systems. As all of these are components of operational risk, it then becomes apparent that an integrated risk management approach needs to focus on operational risk. It needs to ensure that relevant components, systems and infrastructure are in place to measure and monitor market and credit risks on an enterprise-wide basis and that staff are available at all levels of the organization who are able to interpret the outputs and take appropriate actions.

In looking at a corporate level risk framework, the organization needs to ensure that the various key components are in place. These components include organizational issues and people issues such as strategy, structure, people, skills etc. and technological issues such as component systems, communication infrastructure, data warehouses, data mining and risk management tools. The organizational issues include:

- development of a risk management strategy;

- development of risk management culture;

- definition of management roles and responsibilities;

- ensuring that an appropriate management and control structure is in place.

The people issues include:

- the relevant type and calibre of people are available;

- there are adequate levels of training and development of the staff;

- the staff have the skill levels that are appropriate to the tasks assigned to them.

The technology issues include:

- adequate systems to support the various product lines;

- systems are available for management information and reporting;

- there is communication infrastructure to support the operation;

- data warehouses that allow integration and consolidation of information and data across the organization;

- tools and systems available for managing market risk across the organization;

- enterprise-wide credit monitoring and credit risk management systems.

There are four fundamental themes that are critical for establishing and maintaining a comprehensive and effective risk management framework:

- The ultimate responsibility for risk management must be with the board of directors. They need to ensure that organization structure, culture, people and systems are conducive to effective risk management. The requirements for risk management must be defined and established by those charged with overall responsibility for running the business.

- The board and executive management must recognize a wide variety of risk types, and ensure that the control framework adequately covers all of these. As well as including market and credit risks, it should include operations, legal, reputation and human resources risks, that do not readily lend themselves to measurement.

- The support and control functions, such as the back and middle offices, internal audit, compliance, legal, IT and human resources, need to be an integral part of the overall risk management framework.

- Risk management objectives and policies must be a key driver of the overall business strategy, and must be implemented through supporting operational procedures and controls.

The above themes give an indication of the broad scope of the principles, which is critical in underpinning a truly comprehensive risk management framework.

The role of senior management

Boards of directors have ultimate responsibility for the level of risk taken by their institutions. Accordingly, they should approve the overall business strategies and significant policies of their organizations, including those related to managing and taking risks, and should also ensure that senior management is fully capable of managing the activities that their institutions conduct. Global Derivatives Study Group[1] recommends that:

> Policies governing derivatives should be clearly defined. . . .
> Senior management should approve procedures and controls
> to implement these policies and management at all levels
> should enforce them.

Senior management should be able to identify and understand the types of risks inherent in their institution's activities and to ensure that its lines of business are managed and staffed by personnel with knowledge, experience, and expertise consistent with the nature and scope of the organization's trading activities.

The board of directors needs to assess and define the risk appetite for the organization that in turn depends on the risk culture of the firm. There must be a clear statement of the firm's risk philosophy regarding financial risks. It is only when this has been defined, that the institution's senior management can work out the organization's risk profile and formulate the policies and guidelines relating to the management and control of these risks. These policies should cover how and when financial instruments may be used in the broadest terms and must be developed in line with the institution's capital base, its business aims, its risk culture and its overall ability to manage and control risk. These guidelines must be comprehensive in nature and must cover areas of financial policy, credit risk, market risk, legal issues, human resource management, accounting and reporting considerations, as well as culture, organizational structure, management information and internal control systems.

One of the problems is that most boards comprise people who do not have a detailed understanding of financial instruments, especially derivatives. This fact has been demonstrated over and over again in the losses incurred by financial institutions including Barings, Orange County, Procter and Gamble and many others. Until the boards of companies can build up some expertise, the firms are not going to be able manage the risks effectively or react effectively the changing environment. All board members need to understand the risks in their trading and operations that may lead to financial losses. The directors should nominate individuals with defined responsibility for ensuring that there is adequate expertise within the organization for financial instruments being traded. They should be provided with the training and education to ensure they understand the uses and risks of various financial instruments, including derivatives, as well as the problems of their management and control.

One of the key tasks to the senior management is to foster a risk management culture within the organization. Although risk management is the responsibility of the staff at all levels of the organization, there must be an explicit allocation of risk management responsibility among senior managers to ensure management accountability for risk control. Management and staff accountability for risk management can be encouraged through linking reward systems to effective risk management as well as comprehensive annual assessments and reporting on the effectiveness of risk management systems.

The board's commitment to developing and maintaining a risk control system must be reflected in the resources that are made available and the profile of the risk management and control personnel within the organization. The resources must be made available for continued risk management training throughout the organization. Additionally, funds must be made available by the organizations for the development of the hardware and software infrastructure, as well as the recruiting and retention of staff with the appropriate expertise, skill and experience. As well as the responsibility, the board must devolve the authority to the risk management and control personnel to enable them to carry out their tasks. They must have independent access and direct lines of communication with board members.

The linking of the reward systems to effective risk management is another method of developing and nurturing a risk management culture. The organization's compensation policy should not be such as to encourage its risk-takers to take on unnecessary risks. The annual bonus of the trading staff or corporate treasurers should not be entirely based on their profitability but should also take into account the riskiness of their activities, departmental and team performance, and the risk-taker's value-added to non-trading activities. Effective monitoring, control and management of risk should be recognized in the compensation policy.

There should be a continuous monitoring process to ensure the integrity of the risk management controls and systems. While organizations must develop a risk management culture such monitoring and internal and external risk audits have an important role to play in the risk management process. This would involve auditing and testing the risk management process and internal controls and ensuring that the systems, procedures and controls are robust. At a minimum, there should be an annual internal and external risk audit. The risk audit would be a substantial undertaking that would review all the processes associated with measuring, reporting and managing risk. It must evaluate the independence and overall effectiveness of the risk management function and ensure that risk management personnel as well as the trading and risk taking staff are complying with established risk management policies, and that proper documentation on the risk management process and internal controls is in place.

Additionally, there must be a supervisory role (either an individual or a team) to ensure controls and procedures are followed and that senior managers do not override internal controls in their daily operations. There is a requirement for a continuous and systematic identification, testing, and evaluation of critical internal controls to determine their continued applicability and to ensure that established procedures are followed.

Senior management needs to ensure that there is adequate segregation of duties between risk management and control personnel and the trading personnel. The process of measuring, monitoring, controlling and reporting risk exposures should be managed separately from those who generate the activities that bring about the risk. It is up to senior management to decide how this segregation of duties is achieved. Senior managers must clearly define responsibilities between front office and back office. Operations personnel, who are responsible for confirmation and settlement, must maintain a reporting line independent of trading, where the trade execution takes place. The financial industry has been recently reminded of this very essential control, first with Barings and again with Daiwa Bank.

The nature, size, activity, culture and structure of each company is different as is its risk appetite. Additionally, the nature of risk management roles and responsibilities and the types of tools, initiatives, and measurement techniques available to an organization will differ. However, there are a number of underlying principles that will be applicable to all institutions as they formulate policies for the implementation of an integrated approach to operational risk management.

The failure of Barings and trading losses at Morgan Grenfell and Sumitomo Corporation are proof of the need of a new approach to operational risk management in global institutions. Looking at the components of operational risk, the largest proportion of issues arise from problems which the organizations ought to be able to control themselves. The major financial institutions should be looking to develop a global framework for comprehensive and effective management controls. Such a framework must take into account the organization's risk appetite, risk culture, organizational structure and technological infrastructure. However, probably the biggest challenge is for organizations to develop a framework that will allow them to react quickly and flexibly to external shocks and internal breakdowns. In order to develop this flexibility, organizations need to:

- Hire, support and retain staff at all levels of the organization with an appropriate level of skills and expertise.

- Establish training and development programmes that will allow the staff to continuously develop and improve their skills.

- Invest in an enterprise-wide risk-monitoring system, that has the capability to integrate data from the various product line systems to provide a consolidated view of the organization's exposure. The individual product line systems need to encompass sophisticated risk models and have the capacity to handle high-volume, high-speed transactions.

- Establish a management structure with appropriate checks and balances, between front and back office.

- Establish an independent risk management organizational structure.

- Adopt an integrated approach to market, credit risk and operational risks.

It will be this flexibility that will ultimately allow the organization to respond to the changing market and customer requirement.

Risk management culture

The concept of risk management within the financial industry has frequently been associated with financial loss or fraud, e.g. Barings, Sumitomo, Orange County etc. Risk management generally, and operational risk in particular, really comes into focus when something has gone wrong, or when an organization has suffered a substantial loss. As a result of this, there is often a pre-occupation with and excessive focus on administrative processes and controls, rather than outcomes and performance. As the financial business has become more complicated and global, it has generated greater risk management problems. However, because of this fixed mindset and paradigm paralysis, with each new problem, the cry goes up for greater levels of control, more rigid hierarchies and less staff empowerment. Rather than solving any problems, this approach creates fear, uncertainty and suspicion among the staff. This merely serves to drive the problems underground, creating a much bigger risk management nightmare.

Organizations need to break out of this cycle and explore different ways of managing risk. In some cases the term risk management is rather misleading. The process of risk management does not necessarily focus on the management of risk, which is uncertain and unpredictable in nature, but on the capability of the organization to operate effectively in a changing and uncertain environment. Managing risk is actually about managing the organization: planning, organizing, directing, and controlling organization systems, processes and resources to achieve the organization's objectives. Effective risk management requires development of the organization's systems, processes, and resources to change the organization and its responses to the its environment.

The organization needs to develop a risk management culture where risk management is seen as the responsibility of the staff at all levels of the organization. This means that systems and process are designed with risk management in mind and staff development and training focuses on effective risk management practices. The risk management process needs to involve continuous measuring, monitoring and controlling of all risks within the organization. The risk oversight responsibility of the management needs to be clearly defined and communicated.

An organization will only be able to manage risk effectively if its management and staff want to. While the regulators may insist on expensive value at risk type systems or force the organization to develop comprehensive procedures and operational instructions, these activities do not in themselves lead to effective risk management. It is the individuals who have to decide whether they are going to manage operational risk. Because risk management is about asking questions and challenging the establishment, individuals within many institutions feel vulnerable when having to address these issues. For example, an employee working in the back office would feel reluctant to challenge a senior trader or a senior manager about the issue of employee fraud because they risk alienating their own colleagues.

The key risk management guiding principle is to 'embed' risk management into the organizational culture. This means creating a risk-aware organization, a process that typically requires a cultural change to incorporate the idea of risk into every employee's thinking. This requires a shift in the corporate paradigm or mindset. This shift in the mindset and the development of a positive risk culture within the organization requires a fundamental review of the nature and structure of the financial institution. A number of key actions need to take place:

- The board and the senior managers need to demonstrate, through word and action, that they consider risk management a high priority. The oversight responsibility by boards of directors and senior managers within the institution needs to be clearly identified and communicated to all staff. This focus on risk management needs to be reflected in the organization's structure, culture and processes.

- The organizational lines of responsibility and authority need to be established and communicated clearly so that issues can be escalated to appropriate level without any ambiguity.

- The organization needs to take a cross-functional view of risk in order to break down organizational and functional barriers. Functional hierarchies and operational silos can be a breeding ground for unmanaged risks. The enterprise nature of risk means that its effective management requires a business process rather than a functional or a departmental view. Moving to a business process view of the organization involves a massive change not only in the process flow but also the organization culture, management style and staff skill requirement.

- The measurement of risk and exposure on an enterprise-wide basis is a key component of effective risk management. A risk information system that provides consolidated risk data across the organization in a timely fashion would allow the management to adjust the company's risk profile in response to portfolio and market changes. The techniques and tools for measuring market and credit risk are well developed and relatively readily available. Operational risk does not lend itself to the same level of analytical measurement. The nature and scope of operational risk is such that only qualitative and subjective measurements are possible.

- The organization should develop and communicate a clear set corporate objectives and strategies that should include acceptable attitudes to risk taking and the establishment of guidelines within which the various trading and operating units need to function. The goals and objectives of the risk management programme should have been defined and clearly communicated to staff at all levels. The gains from risk management, for the organization and the individual staff, need to be tangible and measurable. This will allow the organization to set group and individual goals.

- In order to promote a positive risk culture, the organization needs to create financial and non-financial incentives that are aligned with risk management objectives. This means that pay structure and bonuses of the staff, including the trading staff, should not only reflect the profitability of the individual or group but also the riskiness of the business and any risk mitigation techniques that were used. This provides incentives for staff to be more aware of the risk that the organization is taking and promotes individual and group accountability and behaviour congruence at all levels of the organization. The non-financial incentives such as promotions or recognition also need to reflect contribution to the risk management process.

- The remuneration structure can also be used to control the risk and investment horizon. If the trading staff's bonus is tied to their profitability and the bonus is paid on 31 December, then the investment and risk horizon is one year on 1 January and only one month on 1 December. If the staff have long-term pay structures, then their investment horizons are also likely to be long term.

- The organization needs to provide support and training for the staff to ensure that they understand and are able to undertake the tasks assigned to them. The staff should also have access to training that goes beyond their immediate functions and even beyond the current needs of the company. This provides tools for the staff to break free of fixed perceptions and to 'think outside the square'. It would open up possibilities beyond the obvious.

- The risk managers should be regarded as a valuable resource that can provide an independent, objective input on matters ranging from overall business strategies to specific projects. The importance of the risk function should be recognized by the organization and this should be reflected in the composition of the board and senior management committees.

- Risk management is not a one-off activity. The organization needs to ensure that there is a process of continuous learning. Risk management is a dynamic and evolving process. A financial institution is in a constant state of change due to the continuous change in the markets, products, customer requirements, regulatory changes, technological advances and organizational developments. The resulting change in the risk profile requires a constant development and evolution of the risk management processes and procedures.

- Organizational processes and procedures should be designed to empower its staff rather than entangle them in red tape and bureaucracy. Many organizations develop procedures in response to regulatory requirements. The main focus of the regulators tends to be to minimize risk rather than necessarily effectively managing it. Organizations should develop and implement procedures that reflect their own priorities and that are in tune with their own corporate goals.

- Success in risk management and development of risk management capabilities should be advertised and promoted within the organization and within the industry generally. This reinforces the management commitment to the importance of effective risk management.

- As the emphasis shifts from 'making money to not losing money', effective operational risk management is an increasingly important function for an investment institution. With effective risk management processes in place, the organization can focus more of its energies and talents on the core of its business, i.e. maximizing the effectiveness of its investment management and client service functions and thus enhancing its prospects for long-term viability.

While effective risk management relies on individual initiative, corporate culture plays a critical role in defining the behavioural norms for an organization. The organizational culture can create an environment that is conducive to risk management by minimizing the personal risks that staff have to take in managing operational risk. An organizational culture that has a positive approach to risk management is likely to promote individual responsibility and accountability. It allows staff to question and challenge the established ways of doing things. This constant review of procedures and processes promotes understanding and helps identify new and better ways of accomplishing the tasks. A positive risk culture allows people to admit that there may be gaps in their knowledge or that they have made a mistake. Cultivation of such honesty in staff at all level allows the organization to take corrective action at the earliest possible opportunity in the event of problems occurring.

The establishment of a risk aware culture within an organization is fundamental to the effective management risk. This requires commitment from the board and senior management, clear definition of strategy, implementation of the policies outlined above and provision of support and training for the staff. Adopting this approach is likely to create substantial change within the organization. The effective management of the transition to the risk aware culture will allow the organization to monitor, control and manage risk while retaining creativity and flexibility.

Enterprise-wide co-ordination

In order to effectively manage enterprise-wide risk, the risk management function needs to have cross-functional responsibility with a direct reporting line to the board of directors. This will allow the co-ordination of risk management across different business units and provide a 'bigger picture', which may be missing from individual business units' management reporting. The responsibilities for this centralized risk management co-ordination role include:

- helping establish and communicate risk policies and principles;

- ensuring that the company adopts a comprehensive approach, one which includes all types of risk;

- managing risk events, including the collection, identification, analysis, resolution, reporting, and prevention of future incidents;

- acting as a clearinghouse for ideas, a forum for communication, and a link between actions and reactions of individual business units to each other and to the corporate vision;

- reporting to the board of directors and executive management.

Managing organizational paradoxes

Paradoxes are inevitable in an ever changing and complex world. Handy[2] states: 'Paradox I now see to be inevitable, endemic and perpetual. The more turbulent the times, the more complex the world, the more the paradoxes'. Handy identifies nine principal paradoxes that inflict society and that need to be managed. One of the nine paradoxes outlined by Handy is 'the paradox of the organization'. In managing operational risk, it is key that management recognize the organizational paradox and put into place policies and procedures to manage it. It should be noted that it is rarely possible to completely solve these paradoxes; however, the inconsistencies can be minimized and some of the contradictions can be reduced. As Handy suggests 'Paradoxes are like the weather, something to be lived with, not solved, the worst aspects mitigated, the best enjoyed and used as the clues to the way forward.'

In order to manage risk efficiently and effectively, managers within financial institutions need to be able to identify these paradoxes and manage these contradictions and inconsistencies. Managing the paradoxes means ability to reconcile issues that appear contradictory. Organizations need to be global and local at the same time; they need to be centralized for some aspects and federal in others; they have to be planned and yet flexible. The management needs to be more controlling and more delegating. The employees need to be more autonomous and yet be more of a team. All these paradoxes tend to be present in all organizations to a varying degree. However, successful organizations tend to be able to manage these paradoxes much more effectively.

The paradox of globalization

The nature of financial markets is driving investment institutions towards globalization. This trend is underpinned by the global nature of financial products and services, increasing global presence of the clients and advances in technology and telecommunication. This allows institutions to take advantage of efficiencies at corporate levels by consolidating operations and back-office functions into regional hubs. However, greater focus on customer services within financial institutions means it is no longer acceptable to provide a standard product or service across all clients and regions. Each institution needs to differentiate its products by providing a bespoke service to meet the needs and expectations of its customers at various geographical locations. In short organizations need to be global, to gain operational efficiencies, as well as being local, to provide a bespoke service.

Organizations need to 'think global, act local' to manage this paradox. They will require a global infrastructure to take advantage of the economies of scale at the corporate level while developing strong local management teams responsible for customers. The corporate centre will provide the cohesion and develop shared values while retaining a fast, more focused and flexible approach of a small organization to service the local market requirements. Organization will need to become more decentralized and federal in nature to cater for this. There is also likely to be a refocus on 'core business' with non-core activities being out-sourced or subcontracted. Vertical integration, where companies try to bring all parts of the business under central control, needs to give way to decentralization and companies forming close and mutually beneficial relationships with other organizations. Figure 7.1 shows an outline of a flexible organization.

In this flexible organization the ever-shrinking core function of an organization is supplemented more and more by external, part-time resources, either in the form of outsourcing, subcontracting or short-term contracts.

Rapid technological change, more intensive competition, shorter product life cycles and more specialized markets have highlighted

Figure 7.1 The flexible organization.

the liabilities of large-scale vertical organizations. There is therefore a move towards various kinds of decentralization, inter-firm agreements, collaborations and partnerships as organizations join together to create global strategic alliances. This co-operation based framework for business activity leads to much closer ties and greater sharing of resources and information between organizations, enabling greater efficiency, flexibility and innovation to respond to market requirements. These relationships are sometimes referred to as strategic networks and defined as 'long term relationships among distinct organizations that allow them to sustain a competitive advantage against their competitors outside the network'.[1]

However, as the organizations become more decentralized and more flexible, it requires a greater degree of monitoring and control to manage operational risk. This leads to the second main paradox.

The paradox of control

The requirement within financial markets is for a greater level of monitoring and tighter controls to ensure that disasters of the past few years (e.g. collapse of Barings, losses at Sumitomo etc.) cannot happen again. However, as businesses become more complex, diversified and more decentralized, there is greater devolution of power from the centre to the local operations. This more federalist approach means that the centre effectively has less direct control of the operation in the satellite offices. The paradox that needs to be managed is less direct control but greater effective monitoring.

One possible paradox of risk management lies in the devolution of decision-making to employees through the 'empowerment process'. This may give rise to new risks. Newly empowered employees and operating units may undertake activities and actions unanticipated by senior management, some of which may create problems and harm for the organization. The organizations have to develop strategies to combat these additional risks. One solution for this is to build a risk-aware culture within the organization with a stronger sense of risk awareness and ownership at employee and unit levels. There need to be some objectives and 'ground rules' defined to ensure that the risk taking is kept within acceptable boundaries. However, the management need to ensure that creativity is not compromised through excessive control. The move towards decentralization, coupled with risk aware organizational culture, means both creativity and strong risk management can flourish within the organization.

This federalist approach cannot work without a strong centre. Traditionally a strong centre meant that a lot of people had to be employed to co-ordinate, plan and monitor activities of the satellite offices. This concentrated an even greater amount of power in one place. However, advances in technology and the information revolution mean that the centre can now be small, well informed and dispersed. With the right technology infrastructure and management information and decision support systems, managers can closely monitor the business remotely. The data for the decision support systems can be sourced independently to minimize the risk of data errors or fraud. Using independent sources of data ensures that the risk of the type of fraud perpetrated by Nick Leeson when he did not report the huge losses on the error account (i.e. the 88888 account) is minimized.

The paradox of work flexibility

There is growth in flexible working; individuals look to change their jobs many times through their careers; and more work is being handled on a temporary basis with teams assembled just for current projects. However, the global nature of the financial markets means that it is now a round-the-clock business. Individuals have to work extremely long hours to cover the various time zones. There is pressure on the operations department to ensure that all the processing for all the markets is completed and the information is available to the client as soon as possible. This information includes all the business transacted, market prices, interest rates, exchange rates as well as revaluation, profit and loss calculation and cash movements. Additionally there is an increasing regulatory and management pressure to increase the levels of monitoring and control of the business. These contradictory pressures of greater work flexibility and more control need to be managed within organizations.

The continuing trend towards the development of modified matrix and project based organizations allows multi-disciplined teams to have maximum autonomy and responsibility and set their own goals and targets. These team cells can then manage their own time and set the pace for themselves. The technological infrastructure allows the management to monitor the outputs and consolidate the information across teams on an enterprise-wide basis in a timely fashion. This will allow the organization to reconcile the requirements of greater individual flexibility and more effective monitoring of the business.

Toward a more flexible organization

The last few years have seen many changes in the structure and culture of organizations. Before the 1970s the work environment was relatively stable and structured; people and their careers were relatively organized; problems and their solutions were well defined and employment tended to be for life. The industrial landscape was dominated by large multinational manufacturing giants like General Motors and Ford whose hierarchical organizational structures had been defined in the 1930s. The successive oil crises of the 1970s, development of new technology and the demand for increased productivity led to a rationalization of the manufacturing industry. Technology enabled organizations to automate the manufacturing processes resulting in substantial job losses at operational levels. During the 1980s and early 1990s the focus shifted from the manufacturing to service industries. With further developments in technology and increasing availability of management information, organizations began to look at their own set-ups with a view to rationalizing the hierarchical structure. The subsequent organizational changes led to a large number of job losses among middle management. Today this trend is continuing, organizations are becoming more flexible, work is becoming increasingly global and the management much more decentralized and devolved.

The investment banking industry has seen substantial changes over the past two decades. However, the conservative nature of the banking environment has meant that the industry has been slow to adopt some of the recent management and organizational development techniques. One consequence of this has been that financial institutions have been trying to manage their complex, expanding and rapidly changing businesses with inappropriate organizational models and cultural frameworks. The industry needs to update its operating models, moving away from functional models to a more customer orientated approach and to take advantage of the opportunities offered by developments in technology and telecommunications.

It is surprising to note that despite tremendous advances in technology and management techniques, the management models most frequently found within financial institutions are still based on the scientific management techniques developed by F.W. Taylor at the beginning of the twentieth century. The main principle of scientific management is that a business process can be subdivided into its constituent parts and an individual can then perform each part. This was revolutionary thinking in the 1900s and had a tremendous impact on the work environment. The implementation of scientific management techniques led to a number of developments:

- The focus moved away from skilled craftsmen and general-purpose tools to specialist single purpose machines with 'skills' built in the machine. There was a general de-skilling of the workforce and move toward semi-skilled labour.

- In order to achieve increased efficiencies, the jobs were broken down into their constituent parts and standardized. The time and motion studies carried out helped define the optimum way to complete each task.

- The system became of paramount importance and control was seen as fundamental to all good design and efficient operation.

- The planning was with the managers; workers merely carried out the tasks.

Looking at financial institution today, it is rather disappointing to note that many of these characteristics can still be frequently found in many areas, particularly within the operations function. Although technology has begun to eliminate some of the rather manual processes within banks and financial institutions, the operating models still owe more to scientific management than to the more human-resource-management and customer-focused models.

In order to meet the challenges of today's competitive environment and to manage the paradoxes outlined above, the industry needs to move on from these outdated concepts and adopt a more customer-orientated approach. Organizations need to focus more on business processes rather than individual tasks; they need to develop and train their staff and put in place infrastructures that will allow them to tap into the capabilities and expertise of their staff at all levels of the organization.

Note

1 Jarrillo, J.C., On Strategic Networks, *Strategic Management Journal*, Vol. 9.

8 | Business process reengineering

One of the techniques that is available to management for gaining substantial operational improvement is business process reengineering (BPR). The technique was developed at MIT and popularized by Michael Hammer.[1] BPR fundamentally differs from the scientific management approach; whereas scientific management concentrated on the optimizing functional tasks, BPR aims to deliver dramatic improvements in response time, service and quality by focusing on customer orientated business process.

The development in information technology has allowed organizations to start the process of integrating various functions within the organization as well as between different organizations. Many organizations are beginning to use IT and their IT infrastructure to gain a competitive advantage. The requirement for sharing data and information between financial institutions, markets, clients as well as regulatory agencies has meant that organizational boundaries are much more permeable to IT. These electronic links allow organizations to share information and thus can help expand their joint capabilities.

This type of IT-led business integration is leading to the development of virtual organizations that will develop new strategic relationships between institutions and their customers, as well as new relationships with exchanges and the regulators. This shifting of the boundary of the organization out to include elements of other organizations offers an alternative to the strategic options of vertical or horizontal integration. This information exchange and sharing for mutual advantage enables greater efficiency, flexibility and innovation to respond to market requirements.

The impact of increasing competition and the accelerating pace of change in terms of globalization of the marketplace and economic and competitive pressures is forcing institutions to seek fundamental changes to improving performance. One way to do this is to adopt a more integrated approach that allows organizations to link competitive strategy, business processes and supporting technologies.

An organization's business process perspective cuts across the functional, departmental or product boundaries, to look at key business processes. These processes are defined as a structured set of activities that produce a specified output. In looking at each key business process, the organization must assess its relevance to the overall business strategy. This is a fundamental review of all the business processes, and will involve massive change, not only in process flows, but also in organizational power and controls, skill requirements, reporting relationships and management practices. This strategic perspective implies wide-ranging radical change that needs careful management consideration. Therefore it is imperative that senior management are able to allocate the time and effort necessary to drive this activity.

BPR can be seen as the culmination of a number of techniques that provide operational efficiencies and process improvement. The techniques include product improvements, total quality management (TQM) and restructuring. Whereas these other techniques provide incremental improvements around the existing organizational framework, BPR is a much more radical approach that looks for the organization to re-invent the way it does business. The golden rule of BPR is 'be bold, think big'. BPR is not about automating or optimizing existing processes, it is about a fundamental review of whether the process adds value or is necessary. BRR provides a common set of tools to meet the challenges set by a greater focus on customers who demand bespoke service and products, competitors and the accelerating pace of change that is requiring organizations to be innovative and proactive.

Benefits of BPR

The substantial benefits gained from BPR are particularly significant for customer service, cost management and staff empowerment.

Customer service

Improved responsiveness to customers of the process, whether inside the organization or out, is perhaps the most important benefit of BPR. Quality and speed of service are improved because people at the interface with the customer are given the responsibility and authority to act. They do not have to refer to some higher authority for agreement, or even pass customer to a series of further contact points.

Cost management

Cost reduction can be achieved by eliminating unnecessary work by simplifying workflow. Traditionally, work passes along a process in batches from one specialist group to another, as shown in Figure 8.1. Where problems occur, these are referred to managers who are effectively experts in that particular activity.

In Figure 8.1, the dotted line shows the process workflow. A, B and C are separate functional departments. The responsibility for the process passes from department to department. In this scenario, departments A and B will have little say in the final product or service delivered by department C, which will be seen as the owner of the final product/service despite not having had any responsibility for the initial stages of the process. The response time for resolving problems is likely to be slow because:

● there is lack clear ownership or responsibility for the whole process; and

Benefits of BPR

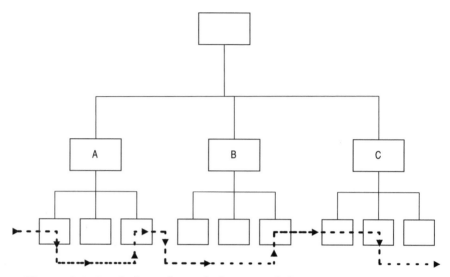

Figure 8.1 Work flow through functional departments.

- problems are likely to be passed around various departments and sections.

However, after BPR, an individual or a team will carry out the work for the entire business process. Staff will have the authority to take action beyond the previous functional levels and will be given training, education and the information necessary to fulfil the overall needs of the process.

Staff empowerment

Enrichment of the working life of the staff involved in the new role is the third benefit of BPR. Staff get greater satisfaction from catering for the needs of 'their customers' than they do from being just one part of an overall process. As they are less dependent on other people, they are able to monitor and control their own work. They also know that if something goes wrong they are the ones that will have to sort out the problem. There is therefore more incentive to 'get things right first time'. Quality and service become personal issues, and for the staff, work becomes more meaningful.

To gain maximum benefit from BPR, the organization has to be committed to the process. However, once the regime is established, the process of improvement can be iterative.

BPR processes

BPR is a fundamental shift in the way of doing business. It rejects the task-orientated approach and attempts to find new ways of accomplishing work, which is now organized around customer requirements and outcomes. It is therefore essential that there is absolute management commitment to the process. BPR provides a more customer focused approach and it is instrumental in breaking down functional and departmental barriers.

Figure 8.2 outlines some of the stages that need to be addressed during a business process-reengineering programme. The key process is to establish the objectives. Defining objectives is a powerful way to change organizations. To do this, the managers have to fundamentally challenge their current way of doing things. The objectives need to be radical and aim for quantum leaps in performance rather than incremental change. Many BPR projects

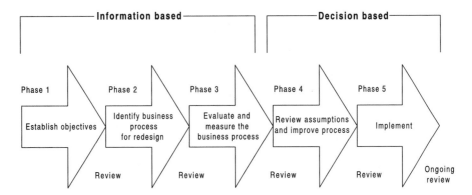

Figure 8.2 BPR processes.

BPR processes

have failed to meet the expectations because managers have been cautious and 'too reasonable' in setting objectives.

The process assessment stage looks at the business, the people and the process itself. The result of the assessment is a rating that indicates the type and scope of the activity that is most appropriate to meet the defined objectives. It will further refine the requirements and allow the organization to target resources to the business infrastructure, development of the staff or reengineering the processes. Figure 8.3 outlines the process assessment framework.

The next stage is to identify processes for redesign and establish their customers and owners. The process should be defined in terms of its beginning and end points and in relation to functions and departments involved. The most important attribute of the

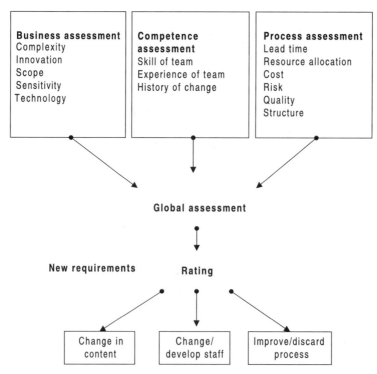

Figure 8.3 Process assessment framework.[2]

process is its customer, whether internal or external, and their requirements. The owner of the process needs to have the responsibility and the authority over the events that take place in the whole process.

In evaluating and measuring the process, it is necessary to understand the problems and identify the bottlenecks so as to provide a yardstick to measure any improvements. However, the objective is to be radical in defining solutions rather than incremental improvements.

The organization needs to consider all options in looking for solutions. The role of technology and information systems needs to be assessed in process re-design. The implementation phase is key to the whole process. There is likely to be a substantial change in both the organizational structure and the role of the individuals. BPR is already regarded as a euphemism for firing staff and is tainted with 'downsizing'. Management needs to ensure that the workforce is kept informed and that staff have the skills, training and the infrastructure to do their new jobs.

Case study – ABC Futures

ABC Futures is a separate legal entity within an investment bank. It provides the settlement support for a substantial house-trading book but is now looking to extend this to provide global clearing and settlement services to its clients. The external client base is primarily UK insurance companies and fund management institutions. ABC Futures uses a clearing and settlement system, which provides adequate functionality for its house operation. There is concern over the level of service that is being provided to the external clients.

ABC Futures is interested in improving the services to the clients and also to add value to its client offering in order to gain a competitive advantage in the marketplace. In order to do this the

Case study – ABC Futures

company needs to understand the requirement of its clients and how they may fit with its current capabilities. The sales team has been talking to the clients and is keen to improve the service.

ABC Futures engaged an external consultant to conduct a client survey and to determine the primary requirement. After analysing the data, ABC Futures determined that 'timely and accurate access to the information' was the prime concern of the majority of its clients.

The initial meeting between the sales team and the senior management to discuss the results of the survey failed to identify the processes that needed to be developed or improved in order to meet the requirements. The management knew that unless they understood and selected the correct processes for development or improvement, the chances of implementing the optimum solution using a hit and miss approach were remote.

The management decided to institute a multifunctional project team to look at all the aspects of the project and define a way forward. Since the team was assembled from the different areas within the operation, they brought with them their own distinctive perspective. The goal of the team was to define or improve the processes involved with providing 'timely and accurate access to the data'. They needed to consider the following:

Definition

- Identifying the clients.

- Understand the client requirements.

- Determine the processes that need to be improved.

- Prioritise the work.

Implementation

- Make the required changes to the process.

- Test the new processes.

- Implement the improvements.

Measurement

- Establish a measurement methodology.

- Continuously monitor and improve.

The team consisted of:

- Jason – client services (team leader)

- Brian – sales

- John – processing

- Fiona – reconciliation

- Bill – treasury

- Adil – information technology.

Phase 1 – Definition

In any project this is the most critical phase. This defines your understanding of the requirements, outlines the processes that need to be changed and determines the nature of these changes. If you select the wrong processes, the 'improvements' may add no value or indeed could be detrimental to your operation. The requirement is to improve service to the clients so you need to ask them what their expectations are and use this information to focus on the processes that may require change. However, before this can be achieved there is a need to identify the clients.

Identifying the clients

ABC Futures team's first task is to identify all the internal and external clients and who would benefit from the 'timely and accurate access to the data'. The external clients are fairly straightforward to identify and Brian (sales) and Jason (client services) have a list of these. Identifying the internal clients is a bit more involved. During the subsequent brainstorming the following list of client groups emerged:

External clients

- institutional fund managers

- insurance companies

- individuals

Internal clients

- management

- compliance

- risk management

- treasury department

- regulatory reporting

The team then ranked these clients in order of importance. Since the project was instigated for providing a global clearing service, external clients were deemed to be the most important. Further work by the team narrowed the focus further to institutional fund managers (IFMs). The team then produced and ranked a list of IFMs based on type of business, volume, and corporate strategy. This produced the top six IFMs.

Understanding client requirements

The team's next task was to determine the requirement. The team felt that the current definition of the requirement, i.e. to provide 'timely and accurate access to the data', was ambiguous and open to differing interpretations. They needed full understanding of the clients' needs and expectations.

Understanding and meeting client requirements is the process of matching your output, whether this is a service or a product, to the client's needs and expectations. First of all you need to define the broad areas of requirement. As some of the team members were internal clients for the data, they were able to define the primary areas of requirements, which included:

- timeliness;

- accuracy of information;

- responsiveness of the staff;

- knowledge of the staff;

- reliability of the systems and data.

The team was aware that these were very broad areas of requirements but they knew that when Bill, Adil and Jason interviewed the clients they would learn the details of their needs and expectations. These interviews will also provide a much clearer picture of the client's key requirements as well as details of their needs. Having identified the general areas of requirements, you can formulate a strategy for client interviews. You should:

- be clear of the information you need;

- keep questions short and to the point;

- document the client responses;

- understand the clients' needs and expectations.

Clients were happy to co-operate and were pleased by ABC Futures' interest in soliciting their opinions and feedback.

Having collected the data, the team was able to analyse all the returns. This produced the list of clients' requirements:

- on-line access to the positions during the day;

- download of the trading data to the clients' office;

- ability to integrate this data with internal systems;

- automatic generation of the daily management and front and back office reports;

- position reports;

- profit/loss reports;

- management summary reports;

- production of weekly trading reports;

- production of the monthly reports;

- reports to be available at 08:00 every morning;

- access to staff in case of problems.

Determining the processes that need to be developed or improved

Having understood the client requirements in detail, ABC were in a position to identify the processes that need to be either defined or improved. This is a very important phase as selecting the right process is crucial to the success of the project. The team identified all the processes that affect the client requirements. It was agreed that the majority of the requirements focused on the extraction of the data from the core settlement system and making it available to the clients. There were further processes for producing the reports in the clients' offices and also archiving the data to produce the weekly and monthly reports. It was therefore decided to pass this problem to a more IT focused team with the project team having a watching brief to ensure that the clients' requirements are met. The project team now becomes the internal client for this project.

The IT team produced the following list of process that related to the current requirements:

- trade input process;

- extract data from the core settlement system;

- delivery of data to the client;

- generation of the daily reports;

- data archiving process;

- generation of the weekly reports;

- generation of the monthly reports;

- data integration process.

After the possible list of processes has been completed, the teams were in a position to review the situation and prioritize the developments. All additional factors should be identified and reviewed. For the current project these factors included:

- cost;

- level of control;

- probability of success;

- benefits to the organization;

- importance to clients;

- interrelationship between processes.

Where the processes are independent, developments can be prioritized. However, where the various process are linked, as most of them are in this case, then the interdependencies need to be understood when prioritizing the work. As all the process cannot be addressed at once, the project team decided that the following processes will be developed or improved in the first phase:

- trade input process;

- extracting data from the core settlement system;

- delivery of data to the client;

- generation of the daily reports.

Where the process already exists, as the case with the trade input process, there is a need to analyse and understand how the process currently works. Only then can improvements be defined. All the tasks need to be defined and mapped. Wherever possible, create a process flow diagram to create a graphic view of how the process currently works.

The project team listed the following tasks associated with trade input process:

- Client's front office phones order to ABC Futures salesman.

- Client's front office passes details to its back office.

- ABC Futures salesperson relays the order to the market floor.

- Trade transacted on the trading floor and details confirmed to the salesperson.

- Trade is entered into the exchange system with details of the counterparty. Once matched, the details are registered in the clearing system.

- In ABC Futures back office, trade details are recorded in the clearing system and checked against the ticket from the salesperson.

- Upon agreement the trade is entered in the ABC Futures core settlement system.

- A statement is produced and sent to the client.

- Client's back office reconciles the statement with its own records.

- Resolve any discrepancies.

Having defined the tasks for the process it is important to establish an initial baseline performance measure for the process and highlight any gaps. For the project team the timeliness and accuracy of the data are the two most important requirements that the clients identified. It is possible to gather this data for the trade input process, i.e. the time it took from the client placing the order to when the trade is available in the settlement system and also the average number of mistakes in trade during each day. These baseline measurements can be used in performance comparisons at a later stage.

This type of evaluation is also a good tool to highlight any potential problem areas. Areas within the operation's function that may contribute to these types of trade processing errors include:

- lack of effective controls;

- lack of clear procedures;

- poorly trained staff;

- system functionality missing;

- lack of automation;

- poor communication;

- fear of fraud.

Although each process may have a different problem area, it is possible compare all the major tasks within the defined process (e.g. trade input) against the listed problem areas. This can then be used in the implementation phase to improve the service to the clients.

When developing new processes – such as extracting data from the core settlement system, delivering data to the client and generating the daily reports – ensure that the tasks are documented in detail and checked against the client expectations.

Phase 2 – Implementation

Once the client requirements have been defined and the processes that require development or amendment identified, you are now in a position to set improvement goals and implement the changes. It is important that you are able to set clearly identifiable goals. The advantage of setting specific goals is that you remain focused and results orientated. It also provides opportunities for recognition of your efforts.

In setting your goals review the clients' requirement data. You should be prepared to conduct additional interviews to determine exactly what your clients expect of you. When it is not possible to meet the client requirements entirely, then set an incremental goal, but always keep your clients involved.

The project team decided that the prime objective was to develop the infrastructure to extract and deliver the information into the clients' environment. The secondary objective was to develop the daily reports that had been highlighted. The third objective was to develop the periodic (weekly and monthly) reports.

In setting goals and time scales ensure that:

- You are setting goals that meet your clients' expectations.

- You have provided realistic estimates of the effort.

- All your clients are aware of the changes and how they might impact the current set-up.

- You have the infrastructure (both technology and people) in place to deliver the solutions.

- If you are proposing incremental improvements, ensure that your clients are aware of what improvements you are delivering and within what timescale.

- Ensure that your clients are aware of any requirement that you are placing on them. (For this project, for example, each client will need access to a PC and a modem to receive the data.)

Before implementing any change or developments, test the new environment thoroughly. You should try to get the clients involved to test the new processes on a trial basis. This also provides an opportunity for early feedback on the improvements that you are proposing. In deciding whether the new environment is providing improvements, always refer back to your clients' needs and expectations and whether these are fulfilled by the solution you are putting in place.

Finally implement the solution. In this case the project team were able to implement the following:

- trade input process;

- extract data from the core settlement system;

- delivery of data to the client;

- generation of the daily reports.

The changes to the trade input process were internal to ABC Futures and involved additional controls and automation. The other process changes were technology based and partly implemented on the client sites.

If you are implementing any processes at the clients' site, you should make sure that:

- They are aware of the operating procedures.

- There is no ambiguity in terms their responsibility.

- There is no ambiguity about support and maintenance.

- There is adequate training provided.

Phase 3 – Measurement

You have now defined your clients' needs and expectations, identified the processes that need to be developed or improved, set priorities and goals and finally implemented the first phase of the solution. But you are not quite finished yet.

For effective improvement in service to your clients, you need to ensure that there is continuous feedback, so that you can gauge what you are doing and whether the changes you have implemented were targeted correctly. It also allows you to continue to offer improvements as their requirement change.

You should communicate the changes that you have implemented, both improved process flows and guidelines, within the organization. They should become part of the company's operating procedures.

The project team reaches its Phase 1 or incremental goal by being able to deliver the data and reports to their clients. They continue to monitor all the tasks associated with the various processes to ensure that ABC Futures is meeting the clients' requirement in the best possible way.

Notes

1 Michael Hammer and James Champy (1993) *Reengineering the Corporation*, HarperCollins, New York.
2 Regan James (1995) *Crunch Time – How to Reengineer Your Organisation*, Century Business.

9 | The learning organization

The pace of change has been accelerating throughout the 1990s. The main drivers for change have been globalization, higher customer expectations, greater competitive pressures and developments in technology. In order to meet these challenges and prosper in this new environment, organizations have to develop new operating models and adopt new management techniques. Major reasons for organizational failures include:

- failure to improve process;

- repetition of previous mistakes, i.e. the organizations are unable to learn from past mistakes;

- failure to react to changing market requirements;

- failure to adapt to customer needs.

By implementing organizational learning model, financial institutions can adapt to change, avoid repeating past mistakes, retain critical knowledge within the organization and gain a competitive advantage.

One of the key organizational development techniques that an organization can use in order to gain a competitive advantage is to transform itself into a learning organization. A learning organization is an enterprise that focuses on the continuous improvement of its processes, products, and services; that adopts a cultural paradigm to facilitate the learning of all its staff, both individually and as teams; that embraces continuous change in order to meet its strategic goals.

Financial institutions can gain a competitive edge in the marketplace by creating learning cultures within their organizations. A learning organization is able to develop its human resources to achieve their full potential, and uses learning as a means of improving its business performance and competitive advantage. It is no longer sufficient to have one person or select groups learning for the whole organization. The organization that will be successful in the future will be the one that discovers how to tap people's commitment and capacity to learn at all levels. An organization will gain substantial competitive advantage by being able to learn faster than its competitors.

A learning organization creates an organizational culture in which employees are encouraged to take responsibility for their own development, and are allowed to take part in decisions about it. The employees are given access to support and training which goes beyond the requirements of their immediate functions as well as the requirement to achieve the current business objectives of the company.

Why become a learning organization?

While organizational learning, albeit on an informal basis, has always been part of managing a company, the need for formal and institutionalized learning is a more recent phenomenon. The business environment is becoming more competitive, and increasingly changeable. For financial institutions to thrive they must meet this double challenge and find ways of making their businesses more competitive, and to adapt to rapid changes.

The drive for globalization, the advances in technology and higher expectations from customers are creating an atmosphere of continuous change and higher levels of competitiveness. An organization's ability to understand its environment, assimilate new ideas and to develop action plans faster than its competitors will be the key to its competitive advantage. As organizations become more integrated and the consequences of change become more far reaching, it is no longer appropriate to rely on individuals or small teams to manage change.

The nature of work and the workplace have changed over the past few years. In today's information society, information management and knowledge have become central to competitiveness. There is a greater reliance on knowledge workers. Therefore continuous learning by individuals, teams and organizations needs to become part of the working life.

Staff are often the largest item of investment in an organization and this is particularly so in financial markets where the nature of the environment means that staff who can react flexibly to changing situations are essential to the running of the business. It makes commercial sense to try and achieve the maximum return on this investment in human resources. In order to achieve this, individuals need to be motivated and encouraged to fulfil their potential, and make their greatest possible contribution to meeting the needs of the customer. Organizations can gain competitive advantage by getting the most out of their human resources, and, by encouraging staff to learn, they can make the workforce better equipped to cope with change. Organizations who have adopted the idea of the learning organization have found that employee performance improves in:

- staff motivation and confidence;

- improved communication;

- product/service innovation;

- employee creativity;

- coping with change;

- improved customer service; and

- increased competitiveness.

All these improvements have a positive effect on business performance, and, by improving the skills and knowledge of the workforce, a company can maximize the return in its investment and gain a competitive advantage in the marketplace.

Creating a learning organization

There isn't a single way of becoming a learning organization that is right for all organizations at all times. There are several possible ways of implementing these principles, depending on the circumstances of the organization, and the business environment it operates in.

An organization's ability to learn is intimately liked to its culture and its ability to challenge its current mindset. Senior management need to appreciate that creating a learning organization requires a fundamental change in organizational thinking and learning issues need to be addressed as part of all strategic decisions.

A learning organization is adaptable and flexible, ethically aware, focuses resources on training and development, listens to all its staff and acts like a single unit. The leaders of such organizations are stewards, teachers and facilitators. They are responsible for building the organization where people continually expand their capabilities to understand complexity, clarify vision and improve the mental models and corporate mindset.

A learning culture cannot be imposed on an organization from the outside. All of the organization's attributes need to be tuned for the learning process. These attributes include:

- organizational structure;
- organizational culture;
- people;
- processes and systems;
- strategy; and
- control and procedures.

Creating learning organizations requires a change in strategic thinking, development and training of the staff and redesign of organizational hierarchies. There are a number of characteristics and practices that can be developed within an organization that would facilitate a learning culture.

In today's global, technologically advanced and customer focused institutions, change is inevitable. The success of a financial institution depends on its ability to manage change. In the fast paced and increasingly electronic financial environment, resilience to change is probably the most important asset. A learning organization needs to embrace change and thrive on it. Organizations need to develop staff who are focused; are flexible in responding to uncertainty; can manage ambiguity in a structured way; and are proactive in managing change rather than reacting to it.

The management and the organizational culture should encourage and promote an experimental mindset. Individuals and teams must be able to question all aspects of the business and venture into uncharted waters. Failures and successes have important lessons for the organization. There should be mechanisms to store the information about failures and successes; this can form the basis for future decision making. Experimentation also provides the mechanism for fundamentally questioning and testing the corporate mindset and assumptions; this provides a better understanding of the key drivers and their interrelationships.

With organizations becoming more decentralized and federal in nature and companies forming close and mutually beneficial relationships with other organizations, there are opportunities for financial institutions to learn externally, from their customers or partners and internally from their employees. There is a need to move away from the 'not invented here' syndrome and towards using the best available ideas. Benchmarking is a technique that is often used for external learning. Benchmarking involves:

● Learning about your own practices, strengths and weaknesses.

- Seeking out a wide range of other organizations that you may think you can learn from and understanding what are the best available options and processes.

- Rather than merely copying the practices of other organizations, there is a need to build on and adapt these processes to create solutions more suited to your own organization.

- Continuously improve the processes.

Benchmarking allows the organization to identify the gaps between its own processes and the best practice. Rather than incremental improvement in performance, benchmarking offers leapfrog opportunities enabling companies to make dramatic gains. External learning of this type provides a number of distinct advantages for the organization.

- It accelerates the rate of change.

- It can identify break-through improvements.

- It results in improved customer service.

- It can provide competitive advantage.

- It provides a fact-based decision-making process.

- It creates a consensus climate.

The staff within the organization are probably best placed to see the shortcomings with the processes and the actions that need to be taken to improve the operation. With staff empowerment, the organization can tap into this expertise and design more efficient processes. According to Richard Whiteley's 'iceberg of ignorance':

- problems known to the top managers: 4%

- problems known to general supervisors: 9%

- problems known to supervisors: 74%

- problems known to rank-and-file staff: 100%

The mechanisms for disseminating the knowledge quickly and efficiently throughout the organization need to be in place within the organization. The successes and failures need to be assessed and recorded so that they are readily available to the staff. The reward systems need to reflect not only individual and team competencies, but also the contribution made to the learning process.

Systems thinking is the aim and final phase of the organizational learning process. This is achieved when the organization develops processes and procedures to acquire, retrieve, use and communicate organizational knowledge. The essence of systems thinking is to see the organization as a single system that is continuously changing and evolving, and to understand the interrelationships between the people and processes within that system. Figure 9.1 outlines a model for a learning organization. The learning process encompasses individual and team learning, organizational culture and mindset, and aligning of the individual, team and organizational vision. It is only when all these disciplines work together in an interrelated and interconnected way that systems thinking develops, thus moving the organization towards becoming a learning organization.

Figure 9.1 shows a model for creating a learning organization. Learning can only happen when all the various elements (i.e. people, mindset, structure, vision, strategy, processes and procedures) within an organization work together and are seen as an interrelated and interconnected whole rather than as individual parts. Systems thinking in a learning organization requires the discipline of team learning which in turn requires individual learning as a prerequisite. It is important to align the vision and goals of the organization with those of its staff.

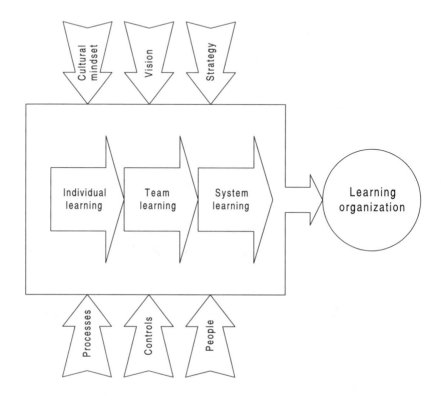

Figure 9.1 Model for creating a learning organization.

Barriers to learning

The structure and culture of many organizations is such that it does not permit enterprise-wide learning. There are a number of barriers that need to be overcome.

- There tends to be great difficulties in moving knowledge across organizational functional boundaries. As most organizations are still structured along functional lines, this tends to create knowledge chimneys where knowledge is not dispersed to the rest of the organization. Additionally functional organizations make it difficult to see the whole picture because the problem is fragmented into many departmental pieces.

- The organizational culture may be too competitive where individuals and teams try to maintain an appearance of a cohesive team while spending their time fighting for turf and avoiding anything that will reflect badly on them. In such an environment people will not admit to the need for learning, as this will be seen as a sign of weakness or incompetence.

- Change can be unsettling. Organizational learning will challenge the existing power structure and threaten current hierarchies. Individuals, teams and interest groups will feel threatened and will develop defensive routines to try to maintain the status quo and stop the organization from learning.

- While there is no substitute for learning from experience, in many cases, people do not directly experience the consequence of their most important decisions. They have either moved on within the organization or left the organization altogether. The emphasis should be on organizational rather than individual learning.

- The organization cannot develop the required cultural mindset, or is slow in the implementation of the strategic change, or is not able to adapt to the technological advances.

Knowledge management

Knowledge management is another technique that is beginning to take hold in the finance industry. In some ways it is similar to the idea of the learning organization in that it tries to tap into and exploit the knowledge and experience held by employees. However, where it differs is that it uses technology to try to capture the knowledge and make it available to other interested parties within the organization. In this way, the company retains the knowledge even after the individual has left the organization. The increasing globalization of the financial services sector, dynamic competition and aggressive use of information technology has changed the way businesses are managed. Although management techniques such as business process reengineering and total quality management have provided a way to control costs by improving operating processes, the tough problems of achieving revenue growth and increased profitability remain. Within increased competitiveness and an accelerating rate of change, organizations need to develop strategies to generate a competitive advantage. Since data and information is becoming a key source of competitive advantage, any technique that allows a financial institution to gather, manage and control information will be of great benefit. Knowledge management has a big role to play in this. For example:

- Know the customer and develop products that are coveted and embraced by them.

- Know the competition to position and price for a profitable sale.

- Know the market and take advantage of the opportunities.

- Know your employees and tap into their knowledge and skills more effectively and mobilize to meet changing demand.

- Know your history and repeat the successes (or at least don't make the same mistake twice).

An organization's knowledge, whether in company's databases, processes or people, is the key asset on the company. The concept is based upon the notion that relevant information, intelligently and quickly communicated to the right person, can make the difference between making great decisions or making bad ones.

Technology is the critical enabler of the knowledge management discipline. Mission critical systems – such as financial reporting, sales automation and resource planning – represent vast stores of legacy knowledge about products, customers and suppliers. Document management applications and data warehouses provide central repositories of information and processes. The Internet, with both its external and internal reach, broadens the available knowledge of markets.

Knowledge is embodied in two distinct forms: explicit knowledge and tacit knowledge. Explicit knowledge can be categorized, stored published and distributed. It includes reports about customer buying behaviour, databases of employee skills and content capturing the latest writing on the latest topic. Most of the knowledge management programmes in place today deal with explicit knowledge. Tacit knowledge is harder to define, harness and disseminate. Tacit knowledge is developed through experience, thinking, observation and intuition. Tacit knowledge is the stuff that we know, and we're not sure why we know it. It also holds immeasurable, indisputable value. This requires companies to exploit the tacit knowledge and skills of the very best people.

Knowledge management success requires a commitment to creating a learning culture. Although formal training programmes are enablers of learning, promoting the sharing of valuable tacit knowledge is invaluable to both financial performance and customer satisfaction.

Before launching a knowledge management programme, an institution needs to understand its objectives and to have an implementation strategy. The project is likely to have the following minimum requirements:

- The organization needs to define objectives and expected results from the knowledge management programme. As part of this project definition phase, the organization needs to articulate and communicate to all its staff what it is hoping to achieve through the knowledge management initiative and define how the success of the programme will be measured.

- The organization will need to define all the information that will be required to satisfy the objective of the programme. It needs to outline the requirements of the business and identify the priority of the various types of information in terms of what is necessary and important and what may only be desirable.

- Th institution needs to identify the sources of the knowledge, both internal and external. There is a huge amount of knowledge commercially available on customers, markets, technological developments as well as economic data on national and international economies. Additionally, there is internal information about resources, expertise and employee skills. As well as this explicit knowledge, there is the tacit knowledge; this is much more difficult to capture and quantify. This is likely to be embedded in the company's processes and procedures and the way that employees do their jobs. Organizations need to tap into this source of knowledge to leverage its skills and experience.

- Collecting or identifying knowledge is not sufficient. The organizations need to create a policy for knowledge distribution. It needs to identify the individuals who need to access the type of knowledge and then make sure that controls and procedures are in place to make the knowledge available to the relevant parties. It is not sufficient to create databases of information and then assume that everyone will access these for their information needs. Knowledge distribution systems need to be part of the organizational processes and procedures to ensure that the right information is made available at the critical phases of the activities. Additionally, organizations need to guard against too such information being made available to its staff. Any security and access implications to the knowledge management system need to be addressed.

- The approach to the implementation of the knowledge management system is critical. The technology requirements to support this programme can be very substantial. Staff at all levels of the organization are likely to require access to the knowledge management system. The technology and the infrastructure needs to be able to support this on an enterprise-wide basis. However, knowledge management is much more than just a technological solution; the technique needs to be embedded into the organization's culture. It needs to be reflected in the procedures, processes as well as the training programmes of the company. Organizations need to develop incentives and forums to encourage staff participation in the programme.

● When launching the knowledge initiative, the management need to ensure that there is commitment for the programme at all levels of the organization and that there is training and ongoing communications for all the staff.

The role of technology in knowledge management

Technology is the critical enabler of knowledge management processes. Technology plays a role in the capture of knowledge, knowledge development, publishing and knowledge distribution.

Knowledge capture

Knowledge represents the sum of many different sources of internal and external information. The sources of explicit information include back-office applications, customer service systems, human resources data, documents and news services. The sources of tacit knowledge are meeting minutes, focus groups, observations and gossip. Technologies for knowledge capture include databases and data warehouses for storing explicit information.

Knowledge development

Once the knowledge is captured, it needs be organized, analysed and categorized according to the requirements of programme. The critical technologies for knowledge development include search engines, data mining algorithms, analytical tools and publishing systems. The purpose and complexity of the knowledge required drives the implementation of knowledge development technology. Simple applications may require only the search and retrieval of explicit database information. More elaborate requirements could include data mining, analysis and custom publishing.

Knowledge distribution

Distributing the appropriate knowledge to the right person, at the right time, is a critical component of any knowledge management solution. Mail systems and database access tools provide rudimentary delivery technology. These technologies are not very discerning and can easily create a situation where the individual workers receive more than their information requirements. However, technologies are becoming available that allow more intelligent targeting, proactive knowledge delivery and flexible access to a wide range of knowledge sources.

Note

1 Whiteley, Richard, *The Customer Driven Company: Moving from Talk to Action*, Business Books, London, pp. 117–18.

10 | Change management

Introduction

The finance industry is going through a period of change and consolidation. There is increasing activity in mergers and acquisitions, creating truly global institutions. The financial markets are a truly global industry where national institutions are no longer insulated from the foreign competition. The drive for globalization has resulted in substantial changes in organizational structure and the technological infrastructure. Organizations need to be able to take advantage of their global presence through economies of scale, yet offer local products and services in response to customer needs. Technological developments and better knowledge management techniques are creating flatter hierarchical structures within the organizations and allowing the individual to work much more flexibly. Competitive pressures are forcing organizations to work closely together through developing strategic alliances and partnerships. The subsequent sharing of information and resources is leading to 'blurring' of organizational and information boundaries. With faster access to data and improved information management techniques, people at all levels of the organization can make better and more informed decisions based on the latest data. This allows the authority and responsibility for operational decisions to be devolved to individuals involved in the process. A process- rather than a task-based approach is beginning to break down functional and departmental structures. Growth in teamwork is leading to project-based structures where individuals with different expertise come together for a specific project; on the completion of the task the team is disbanded and the individuals move to work on other projects.

Introduction

All these pressures and developments are resulting in a tremendous amount of change within the industry. The pace of change is accelerating all the time. The traditional hierarchical and bureaucratic organizational structures are no longer relevant in this changing environment. The change is increasingly complex, rapid and unpredictable. The diversity of knowledge and expertise within financial institutions requires a more humanistic approach to management. The organizations need to be more flexible, adaptive, innovative and entrepreneurial. However, the transition from the old bureaucracy to the new organization will create a lot of uncertainty and can be very disruptive. The management of change is a major source of operational risk and the challenge for organizations is to effectively manage the change while staying competitive through the transition.

The drivers for organizational change have already been highlighted in detail in previous chapters. These include:

- globalisation;

- rapid restructuring of the industry through acquisition and joint ventures;

- technological development;

- organizational developments;

- flexible working;

- the financial industry is a very competitive and continuously evolving environment. New products and services are being developed all the time. With increased use of communications technology and the Internet, there is potential for Internet-based virtual organizations challenging the existing order;

- the need for the organization to be underpinned by an effective risk management framework and culture.

Resistance to change

While the above list identifies the major generic drivers for change, the strength of the various drivers will vary from organization to organization. The challenges of adapting existing business environments to the new model are likely to be unique for each situation. Many challenges face organizations embarking on this change; these include cultural issues, technological problems and organizational inertia. The changes are often met with inherent resistance from those reluctant or unwilling to change. There can be many sources of resistance for the proposed change, including individuals, teams, departments and the organization itself. The resistance can manifest itself overtly through industrial action or covertly through lack of motivation, low morale, increased absenteeism, etc. The major reasons for resistance to change include:

- There is a substantial requirement for additional resources during a period of change. These may include financial resources, time or special expertise or skills. Lack of adequate resources can be a major resistance to change.

- Any change in the workplace carries an element of uncertainty. This brings fear about job losses, loss of earnings, loss of status, or even loss of familiar surroundings. This fear of the unknown can affect individuals at all levels of the organization. However, if there is resistance from the senior management, then the process of change is likely to be difficult.

- Those in positions of power and influence in the organization may see change as a potential threat to their position.

- All organizations have a certain amount of cohesiveness and stability in order to function properly. This in turn leads to the establishment of roles, procedures and processes. This can be a powerful source of resistance within the organization. Highly bureaucratic and hierarchical organizations offer a greater level of resistance than more federal and devolved organizations.

- An organization with a high level of fixed investment in existing infrastructure is likely to experience greater resistance to change.

Introducing change in an organization can be extremely difficult and complex. There needs to a clear strategy for where the organization is going. The management must create a new vision and initiate the change procedures and processes to deliver the required change. The approach required for establishing a successful change management project is likely to be different for each specific organization. However, there are a number of critical success factors common to all environments:

- There needs to be an alignment of the new vision to corporate strategy and business objectives.

- There should be clear commitment from the senior management. The change management project needs to be driven from board level.

- There is a requirement to involve and educate as many people as possible.

- During the transition period, there is likely to be a need for additional support activity to allay people's fears.

- The implementation of change needs to be managed like any other project with clear definition of objectives, scope of work, critical success factors, and the role of individuals.

- Ensure that there is adequate education and communication and that there is effective knowledge transfer to the key players.

- At all stages measure, demonstrate and communicate the progress which has been made.

- To ensure the involvement and adhesion of individuals across the organization, the role of each staff member during the transition and in the post-change organization must be defined.

Within the finance industry, the need for change is now generally recognized. There are many models and strategies for implementing change within the organization. Kurt Lewin proposed a three-step model for organizational change, i.e. unfreezing, changing and refreezing. Lewin argued that before change can take place, the organization's commitment to the current environment must be altered. There must be a realization for the necessity of change. The 'unfreezing' can be done by outlining the shortcomings of the current set-up and creating and communicating a vision for the alternative. Once the situation is unfrozen, the change can take place. Refreezing is the process of making change stick by:

- implementing new systems to support the new way of working;

- introducing controls to check that the change has happened and introduce sanctions that discourage the old behaviour patterns;

- redesigning the reward and motivation structures to reflect the desired staff behaviour;

- supporting change through effective communication, education and training;

- developing realistic time scales for introducing change and allowing time for change to settle.

Force field analysis

Force field analysis is a simple technique that can be used to analyse and plan the changes that need to be introduced. This technique has the added benefit of identifying the major driving forces and the factors and influences that might be providing resistance to change. The central premise of force field analysis is that the current situation is an equilibrium between two sets of forces, i.e. those driving towards change and those providing resistance to change. Change can be introduced by a combination of strengthening the driving forces and weakening the opposing forces. The force field analysis can be spilt into three major stages.

Stage 1 – Creating a vision

This is the 'unfreezing' stage in the Lewin's model. First, define the current situation with its strengths and weaknesses. Define the shortcomings of the current situation to outline why change is necessary. Create a vision for the desired new state.

Stage 2 – Identifying the force for and against change

This stage identifies all forces for and against the proposed change. The forces could include the organization structure, culture, skill and expertise of the staff, the commitment of the management, the needs of particular groups or departments, technological, infrastructure, etc. It is not sufficient just to identify the various forces; you need to analyse their relative strengths and significance and assign weights to them. A pictorial representation of the force filed analysis is given in Figure 10.1.

Figure 10.1 provides a useful tool for easily identifying all the forces that are likely to act on a change process. The length of the arrow in represents the strength of the particular force.

Stage 3 – Identifying the actions

During this stage, you need to identify the actions that may be necessary to achieve the desired results. Change is achieved either by strengthening the driving forces or weakening the restraining forces. For example, if the resisting force is the lack of appropriate

Figure 10.1 Force field analysis.

skills and expertise then a focused training programme will reduce this force. It is important to get some initial movement quickly since if one element in the force field moves the others may move too. Also any success provides a tremendous psychological boost.

Developing commitment

While it may be possible, in some environments, to introduce change as a simple matter of requiring compliance with the new way of doing things, in most cases, the commitment of the staff, their enthusiasm and co-operation are essential to the successful implementation of change. To achieve the required level of commitment, the organization must develop a strategy for the introduction of change that:

- breaks down functional barriers and power groups, and encourages open communication and visibility;

- overcomes sceptical attitudes and lack of enthusiasm;

- creates shared vision and objectives across functional teams;

- ensures the involvement and buy-in of staff at all levels of the organization.

Developing commitment

The strategy must address the three stages of the change management process, i.e. preparing for change, implementing change and post-implementation issues.

Preparing for change

This stage creates the awareness of the change and explains to staff why change is necessary. The managers should be letting staff know that change is coming, the extent of the change and should outline the timescales. Since there will be a higher level of commitment to chosen change rather than imposed change, staff participation at the earliest possible point in the change process is of prime importance. Communications, through staff briefing or individual meetings, should ensure that people understand the implications of change and how it will impact them individually. There should be clarification of the functional roles and responsibilities. Change in the workplace creates uncertainty and can be quite unsettling for individuals. Management should strive to create a positive perception of change through setting up whatever support systems are needed so that staff can get used to the changes. The support facilities or systems at this stage include counselling, demonstrations, coaching and briefings.

Education and training play an important part at this stage of the change process. Management needs to ensure that individuals and teams have the relevant skills and expertise for the new tasks that they are being asked to perform.

Implementing change

This is the stage where the change is implemented and the initial problems and issues are being addressed. Having got the staff ready for change, management needs to ensure that the implementation of the change goes as smoothly as possible and any problems are resolved quickly. There should be control and monitoring systems in place to ensure that change has happened. The behaviour of management is key at this stage of the change process. For example, if the requirement was to implement a risk-aware culture within the organization, then the reward systems and motivational structures should reflect this. The senior managers, particularly those responsible for the trading activity, should actively discourage risky transactions.

Once the change has been implemented and the start-up problems dealt with, management should ensure that the change is working as intended and that there are no unanticipated side effects. The longer-term issues associated with current change processes need to addressed and their impact on other parts of the organization needs to be assessed. There is a requirement for ongoing monitoring to see the level of achievement and making changes and adapting the overall plan as necessary.

Post-implementation issues

The change has now been adopted in the workplace and has become the normal order of things. The new reward and motivation structures are in place to perpetuate it. The old ways of doing things are no longer available. The staff have internalized the change and are committed to making it succeed.

Framework for managing major change

In many ways the management of organizational change is similar to managing operational risk. It requires the synthesis of staff, resources, ideas, systems, procedures and processes. It is only when all the issues are effectively addressed that the organization as a whole will learn new behaviour. Figure 10.2 outlines the framework for managing change.

The change process starts when management or the individuals within the organization realize that there is need for change. The

Framework for managing major change

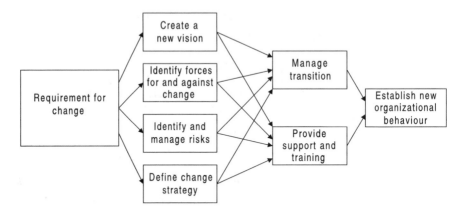

Figure 10.2 Framework for managing major organizational change.

pressure for may be due to declining performance, changing profile of the staff, competitive environment, changes within the industry, merger or acquisition, or technological developments. Whatever the reason for change, there has to be clearly defined reasons for moving the organization from its current state to a new desired state. The advantages of the desired state should be quantifiable and measurable. Initial attempts at alternative ways of working are rarely well received and there is likely to be opposition or even outright hostility to the proposed change.

The management needs to create a vision for change and communicate the necessity for change to staff at all levels of the organization by articulating the strengths and weaknesses of the current situation. They need to assess the various options that may be available and define the best solution for the organization. Wide consultation at this stage would make the eventual adoption of the solution much easier. The benefits of the solution, to both the organization and staff, need to be communicated to all staff. There should be clear and unambiguous strategic vision and consistent leadership from the top management.

The concept of the force field was introduced earlier in this chapter. This technique can be used to identify the major forces for and against the proposed change. Organizational culture and organizational politics can be barriers to change. Management have to assess the motivation of the individuals and groups that oppose change and actively look for ways to mitigate their concerns.

There can be substantial risks involved in any major organizational change. These risks include ineffective management of the change programme, inappropriate change, lack of skills and expertise to work in the new environment, lack of commitment or unforeseen problems. All the risks associated with the change process need to be identified and the issues addressed to minimize the risk potential.

There needs to be a detailed strategy for managing the change process. However, there should be flexibility in the programme to react to and resolve issues and problems as they occur. There should be provision for sufficient resources and capacity to plan, provide logistical support, training and education. The management of the transition is a key activity in the change process. During this phase the organization is learning new behaviour while continuing to work and perform in the existing paradigm. There is a need to provide support and training to help individuals cope with the stress and uncertainty.

While change can be a painful process for organizations and individuals, organizations that fail to change in response to the changing environment will not survive for long in today's competitive markets. The process of change requires the management to react to many different and often seemingly contradictory demands. It creates a great deal of uncertainty among the staff. However, organizations that are able to manage change effectively and learn from the experience are well prepared to meet the challenges of the future.

11 | New role for operations

Having defined a new structure for the company based on the learning organization and knowledge management techniques, optimized the business processes through BPR, empowered the employees and created a risk aware management culture, what is the role for the operations area or the back office?

Figures 5.2 and 5.4 show the central role that the operations function has both in terms of data flows and relationships to counterparties. It is this central role that makes the operations area the ideal starting point for managing risk. The operations area should move away from the traditional administrative support role staffed by young and inexperienced personnel and shed its low skill, 'low tech' image. There needs to be a paradigm shift in terms of the perception of the back office and its role in a modern investment institution. There are a number of developments, technological and business, that are likely to put a greater focus on the operations function and modify its role within the financial institutions. These developments include:

- Technological and system developments have meant that there is less manual trade input and reconciliation in the back office. There is also an increased use of straight-through processing technology and rule-based transactional monitoring systems. This is leading to greater levels of automation within institutions.

- There is a greater focus on enterprise-wide risk management including operational risk. The focus on risk management is shifting form administrative control towards developing a risk management culture.

- There is an explosion of information that is available to organizations and individuals through the Internet, intranets, e-mail, data warehouses, commercial agencies as well national and international agencies. Increasingly it will be companies and individuals that are able to assimilate, analyse and use this information most effectively that will succeed while the rest will struggle to come to term with this.

- The development of learning organizations and knowledge management techniques is leading to information- and knowledge-based organizations. With access to improved information, organizations soon realized that whole layers of management were neither leading nor making decisions. Their sole role appeared to be to act as information relays. With better and more focused information, their roles became redundant, thus creating flatter organizations.

- The role of individuals within the organization in general and in the operations area in particular is evolving. Staff need to develop greater levels of technical and business skills and be prepared to develop and evolve with the needs to the organization. There is greater emphasis on staff development and training.

Given its central location within the organization, and its role as a conduit for information flow, the operations department can play a central role in risk management. With its traditional role of administration substantially reduced due to automation, the back office can make a substantial contribution to the well-being of the company. The organization will be able to leverage the information about its customers, markets and the competitive environment available within the operations area to increase the efficiency of its processes and provide a greater level of customer service.

Additionally, the central role of the operations area allows it to play a crucial role in enterprise-wide risk management. All trading and financial transactions are channelled through the operations area for administration, clearing, settlement and reconciliation.

Additionally, the back office receives market information and prices for revaluation purposes. If the various systems in the operations area can be organized properly, they can be used as the source for a lot of the data that is required for an enterprise-wide risk information system.

While developing a new organizational model for the operations area is no easy task, it is in the interest of the financial institutions to move forward in this area. With greater emphasis on customer service, process efficiencies and risk management, organizations need to develop new strategies for maximizing the return from their investments in the operations area. However, for this to happen, there need to be a number of changes:

- There needs to be paradigm shift in the perception and role of the operations area. The low skill, administrative model for the back office that worked well in the institution of the 1970s and 1980s is no longer applicable in the modern, risk aware and global financial institution. There is an urgent requirement to update and upgrade this organizational model if organizations are to avoid further financial disasters.

- The profile and the perceived value of the operations area needs to be improved. Its key role in the running and well being of the institution needs to be recognized. Organizations need to need to develop reward systems and staff career structures that reflect this new attitude.

- There is no longer any rationale for segmentation of operations functions along product lines. The operations function for the various products, i.e. derivatives, bonds, equities, needs to be consolidated into a single functional area. This will provide better control, monitoring and risk management.

- As the type of work in the back office changes, the type people and the training available to them needs to change substantially. With the focus moving away from administrative support and more towards management of information, the operations professionals need to be knowledgeable about both business and technology.

- As the tasks move from the routine to exception based, there will need to be a greater level of analytical skills within the operations area. Organizations need to invest in training and development of its operations staff to allow them to play a much fuller role within the organization.

- The oganization will need to invest in knowledge management systems to ensure that the capability and commitment of staff is maximized and that the organization as a whole can utilize the knowledge – rather than it being locked within individuals and teams of people.

- The role of the operations area in improved customer service and adding value to the organizations needs to be recognized. As customers begin to focus on efficient operations and control infrastructure as a prerequisite for doing business with a counterparty, an efficient and professional back office can provide the competitive advantage that an institution needs.

The operations function then becomes a key component of corporate risk management and control. Staffed with experts from both the business and from information technology, operations can become the driver for improved efficiency and change within financial institutions. It can add value to the organization through greater monitoring and control of information flow as well providing better and more focused service to its clients.

The result will be improved risk management, more efficient use of information, a more involved and committed workforce providing a competitive advantage in the market.

12 Enterprise-wide risk management

Enterprise-wide risk management is normally regarded as the ability to consolidate market risk across the organization. Senior management often regarded risk management as a matter for financial experts in the corporate treasury department rather than an integrated part of corporate strategy. However, the risk management industry has matured substantially in the late 1990s and now enterprise-wide risk management encompasses market risk, credit risk and operational risk. All the risk categories are interconnected and it is no longer sufficient to for organizations to concentrate on market, credit or operational risks individually. The techniques for measuring market and credit risks are well advanced. The nature of operational risk does not lend itself to quantitative measurements and thus is much more reliant on a pragmatic and hands-on approach to risk management. Indeed, there is a school of thought within the industry that argues that a lot of the losses during the 1990s have been the result of organizations putting too much faith in the mathematical and computer models that have been developed to measure risk. Indeed, some argue that part of today's problems have stemmed from risk managers who have invested too much faith in the statistics and the ability of models to assess risk accurately. As a result, too little attention has been paid to hands-on risk management and the human element in the risk control process. While this may be rather stretching the truth, there is a need to temper the quantitative measurement with a more pragmatic and hands-on approach to risk management.

The risk measurement systems and processes are simply tools and not substitutes for good judgement. It is unprofessional and indeed dangerous to assume that once risk measurement models and systems have been installed the organization can simply stop worrying about risk.

The phrase risk management, particularly when applied to enterprise-wide or operational risk management, can be rather misleading. Risk management is not necessarily about managing risk, which by its nature is unpredictable and uncertain, but managing the organization's ability to effectively deal with uncertainty and to build in certain characteristics to improve its ability to respond to change.

An enterprise-wide risk management system needs to be a combination of risk measurement through robust and integrated systems, organizational culture and structure that is conducive to risk management, adequate levels of controls and procedures, and hands-on control and monitoring by experienced risk managers. This combination would broaden the risk management focus beyond just models, with all staff involved in the management of risk and risk managers constantly evaluating and measuring the institution's risk.

Key components of the overall enterprise-wide risk management system are the risk measurement, data integration, exposure monitoring and management information systems. These systems perform data integration and provide a consolidated view of the potential risks and exposure across the organization.

The role of technology

Technology has a crucial role to play within financial markets. Rather than being 'an enabler', technology is fundamental to the success of companies operating in this area. Technology permeates the entire organizational structure within a financial institution. The information architecture of these organizations includes operational systems, knowledge

The role of technology

systems, management information systems and strategic systems. In functional terms it includes accounting, finance, HRM, sales and marketing, transactional processing, trading, risk management and various types of decision support and executive management systems.

Within the financial institutions, the use of technology is fundamental to the running of the business. A modern financial institution could not function without this technological infrastructure.

While there are risks associated with the use of technology (and technology risk is one of the components of operational risk), technology provides organizations with a backbone along which some of the other organizational developments (e.g. knowledge management, creating a learning organization, developing a risk management culture) can take place. Effective use of technology can provide companies with a competitive advantage.

Technology is now such a fundamental part of transacting business that billions of pounds were spent within the financial markets industry on year 2000 issues. There was a very real danger that companies that failed to find solutions to this problem would be severely affected because their information technology systems no longer functioned.

However, despite all this technology, organizations and technology providers are struggling to provide an adequate enterprise-wide risk management solution. It is appropriate at this stage to make a distinction between the technology needed to support enterprise-wide risk management and that for individual business lines. There are numerous systems and solutions that are available for individual business areas or products, e.g. equities, bonds, OTC derivatives and futures. These systems provide adequate levels of functionality to run these individual businesses. However, there are very few solutions for monitoring and managing risk on an enterprise-wide basis.

Enterprise-wide risk information systems

The variety and complexity of financial instruments traded by most financial institutions means that the assessment, evaluation and control of risk cannot be undertaken without substantial investment in technology. The required level of integration between systems and hardware platforms for enterprise-wide risk management is such that organizations need to develop a corporate strategy for systems and technology procurement. Many organizations do not have a corporate IS strategy; in this scenario each functional area is responsible for its own technology needs with little or no regard for corporate-level integration. This has meant that systems are decentralized, badly co-ordinated that present substantial difficulties when trying to integrate data for risk management purposes. The risks associated with technology have been defined in Chapter 6, Risk spectrum. However, such poorly planned and poorly integrated systems adversely affect the organization's development of an integrated enterprise-wide risk management infrastructure in a number of ways:

- The lack of overall strategy results in piecemeal developments and a focus on short-term needs with little regard for long-term information requirements.

- The quality and integrity of the data is likely to be varied, leading to incomplete or incorrect data. This is unlikely to produce the required information in a timely fashion.

- The lack of system integration will be reflected in the inability to produce consolidated reports for risk management. Senior managers are likely to have to rely on multiple sources of data to get an overall picture of the risk exposure. There will be the additional burden on operational staff of extracting meaningful information from the numerous systems and consolidating it to get meaningful risk information.

- A piecemeal approach to system procurement is unlikely to

provide the flexibility that is required to handle the changing nature of the markets, products and regulatory requirement.

The enterprise-wide risk management system is essential for managing risk across the organization. It has to take data from all the various systems, provide an integrated environment, analytical tools and management reports. It has more in common with knowledge management systems than traditional product based solutions. There are a number of distinct characteristics for this type of system. These include:

- The approach to enterprise-wide risk information systems outlined in this book makes significant use of the existing technology and product-level systems. There is a requirement to utilize this existing functionality by taking feeds of data from these systems into the risk management system. Lack of a comprehensive corporate-level information system strategy means that for most organizations there are many different types of hardware platforms, operating systems and development environments. There is a requirement to receive transactional information from a variety of sources.

- There are very few standards for transactions or interfaces that cover the multitude of instruments and products that are transacted. There are likely to be discrepancies in how different systems handle the same products. The level of details available in the various systems is likely to be different. There is, therefore, a requirement for converting the various type of information into a common and consistent format and storing it in a database so that it can be used for risk assessment purposes.

- There are many sources for the current market data. The sources include information vendors (e.g. Reuters, Telerate etc.), exchanges, commercial databases, models and the Internet. This data needs to be received, validated, and stored for risk management purposes.

- There is a requirement to provide tools for performing the required analysis across all classes of products and taking into account the interaction and correlation between the various classes. These analytical tools would include assessment of current exposure and risk, sensitivity analysis and calculation of profit and loss and consolidation of data for risk reporting purposes.

- The consolidation of data for various product classes is one of the key functions of an enterprise-wide risk system. The calculation of current and future exposures for some of the derivatives instruments can be quite complicated and needs careful consideration.

- The enterprise-wide risk information system will contain the risk profile of the company including financial and position limits for the various levels of the organization. The risk system needs to aggregate the exposure and risks at the various levels, compare these with set limits and highlight any issues or exceptions.

- There needs to be a flexible access to the risk system via reporting and data mining tools. The system should provide flexible reporting of the results for monitoring at various levels of management.

- Underpinning the enterprise-wide risk information system would be a data warehouse that would contain key information about the company's risk appetite and risk profiles.

- The organization needs to ensure that there are comprehensive security measures in place for access to the risk system and the risk data.

This first issue in the development of a risk system is the requirements specification, i.e. to identify the main users and define their data requirements.

The main users of an enterprise wide risk system are likely to be the senior managers, corporate risk managers and risk controllers. The information from an enterprise wide risk system forms the basis for decisions regarding performance, exposure, financial and positions limits and capital allocation. Other information may be used for compliance or regulatory reporting. The key issue is that senior managers, who are the prime users of the enterprise wide risk system do not require the same level of detail as the trading staff or their immediate managers who will have their own risk reporting systems.

Having defined the output data requirement from the enterprise risk system, it is important to adopt an approach that will maximize the use of systems and functionality that would already exist within an institution. Additionally, it is counterproductive, and costly both in terms of financial resources and time, to produce an overly complicated risk system with functionality which is of little use to the target users. The level of functionality, the level of detail, performance and transaction granularity must reflect the target user profile.

The term 'enterprise-wide risk management system' is rather misleading; these types of enterprise-wide systems are not actually risk management systems. They are in fact enterprise-wide risk information systems that provide the necessary information for senior management and the risk managers and help in the decision-making processes. Therefore such systems require processes that are cross-business, cross-customer and cross-product. Data needs to be gathered on all the various activities and systems and converted into a standard format.

Designing an enterprise-wide risk information system is a substantial project for an organization. It is made even more complicated by the requirement to normalize and integrate data from many disparate systems and platforms. Additionally the are many elements to a risk management system including data collection, data normalization and integration, analytic and reporting subsystems.

A key component of a risk information system is the interface layer that acts as an interpreter between disparate systems to convert various messages and data feeds into a common format. This vital middleware system manages the various data feeds providing data collection, conversion and management functionality.

Figure 12.1 outlines a technical framework for building an information system that is needed to manage risk on an enterprise-wide basis. All too often organizations have tried to develop enterprise wide-risk information systems that are built around their existing trading systems without detailed analysis of the requirements, the infrastructure or an understanding of the target users for the risk system. The unsurprising results of such an approach are projects that are over budget, late and do not meet the organization's requirements for risk management information in an accurate or timely fashion.

The framework for the development of an enterprise-wide risk information system has a number of distinct application layers:

- component or product layer

- interface layer

- data integration engine

- data warehouse layer

- client interface layer.

Component or product layer

This primarily contains the technology that is needed to support the individual business lines and would be the major source for the data into the interface layer. This technology is widely available and would be currently in place in most institutions. It

Enterprise-wide risk information systems

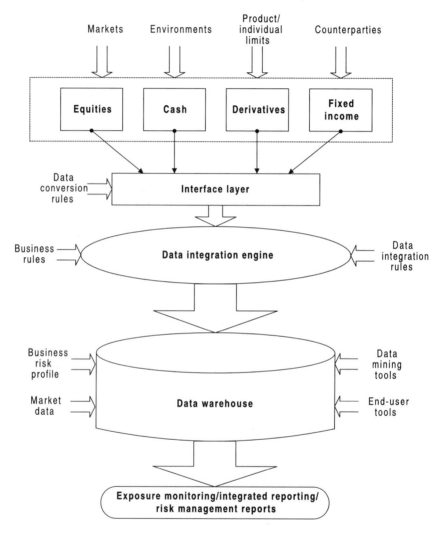

Figure 12.1 Technical framework for enterprise-wide risk management.

includes the company's internal systems for all the products and business lines as well as any external and market data systems. These product- or business-based systems have been described as 'inch-wide, mile-deep' and they possess a product view, not a firm-wide view. An institution will generally have a myriad of systems in support of various products that are traded and may have different systems at different geographical centres. Not only are there many systems, but the various systems may treat the same transaction in different ways. The information may be available in different time frames for global institutions. They all have their own methodologies, data structures and technological environments.

One of the key advantages of the approach adopted in this book for enterprise-wide risk information systems is that organizations can leverage the functionality that exists in the various trading or transaction processing business areas. Organizations do not need to reinvent or replicate the existing product level functionality for enterprise-wide risk systems. The product level positions, revaluation and analytics information can be sourced from the existing systems. Once the data is received from the various business level systems, the risk system can consolidate the results into an enterprise risk profile. This approach simplifies the implementation of the risk system by substantially reducing new functionality that needs to be developed.

Interface layer

Since the data for an enterprise-wide risk information system is typically sourced from many different systems and environments, the quality and the format of data can vary substantially. The first requirement is to normalize this information to produce data in a uniform format. Parsing algorithms can achieve standardization, while more sophisticated techniques using approximate string matching, parsing tables and reference files can be used to further enhance the matching accuracy.

This part of the architecture contains the algorithms for converting the various types of information into a common format and storing it in a database. It also receives and validates current market information from different market vendors or the Internet. The opportunities offered by developments in messaging technologies and electronic data interchange (EDI) makes communication between systems readily achievable leading to greater levels of integration between both internal and external systems.

Data integration engine

This contains all the business models and data integration algorithms as well as tools for performing the required analysis across all classes of products and taking into account the interaction and correlation between the various classes.

Data warehouse layer

The data warehouse is the central database that holds the consolidated risk management data for the organization. This would hold the consolidated risk profiles for the various parts of the organization, market data and rates for revaluation as well as consolidated positions information.

It should be noted that the data held at this level is likely to provide a consolidated view of the organization's exposure and risk. The detailed information of positions and exposure for individual accounts or dealers is likely to be held in the individual business level systems rather than an enterprise-wide risk management system.

Client interface layer

The client interface layer provides the access to all the risk management data via a set of query tools, enquiries and flexible reports.

Underpinning this enterprise-wide risk management system is a corporate communication network that connects all of the institution's assets as well as providing access to external sources of information. The organization needs to ensure that there is sufficient network capacity to handle the increase in data traffic generated by the implementation of an enterprise-wide information system.

Traditionally the overheads of integrating data from so many different systems and sources has been so great as to make this approach unrealistic both in terms of time and expense. However, developments in technology and software tools over the past few years have now made it feasible to attempt data integration at the enterprise-wide level. The use of relational databases and open systems architecture has made access to the core data much easier. The growth in the use of component-based architecture and object-orientated technologies has allowed companies to dissect their business requirements in to discrete modules and develop solutions that can then be integrated to provide an overall solution for the company.

Challenges to enterprise-wide risk management

A number of financial institutions have initiated substantial projects aimed at implementing enterprise-wide risk management. It was estimated that the total spend on these projects was $400 million in 1997 and that this was likely to grow at 20 per cent per year over the subsequent five years. However, there are some technical challenges to enterprise-wide risk management:

- The financial markets will continue to evolve. New products are constantly being developed. There is the on-going consolidation of organizations through mergers and acquisitions. The development in technology and communication is changing the nature of the organizations and their relationship with their staff, customers and competitors. All these changes will continue to affect the nature of risks that are faced by financial institutions. Any enterprise-wide risk information system needs to be able to encompass all these changes. Therefore, flexibility needs to be built into the design of such systems.

- There are a wide variety of component systems that support various business lines. Some of these may have open-system architecture to allow easy access to the data, while others may be legacy systems that may be difficult to interrogate. Whatever the technology or environment, the required data needs to be extracted from these systems and made available to the risk system. There may be some rationalization of the component systems required as part of the risk system project.

- The quality and timing of input data from the component systems may be inconsistent. While some of the component systems may be able to provide real time data, others may only work in batch mode. The data from these latter systems may only be available once a day when the end-of-day batch processing is carried out. Additionally, for a global institution, the time difference between the various geographical locations would need to be taken into account when providing consolidated reports for risk management.

- An enterprise-wide risk information system requires a resilient corporate communication network that has adequate capacity for the additional traffic that may be generated. Trying to implement a system over an unstable network or where there is not sufficient capacity is a recipe for disaster.

- The enterprise-wide risk information framework defines the requirements for such a system. The implementation of this framework would be a very major project for an organization. The development of business models, data integration rules and analytical models and reporting and data mining tools is very complex. The project is likely to involve state-of-the-art technology that may introduce additional technology risks.

- The success of this project depends on meeting the flexibility, speed and accuracy requirements. Provision of accurate data in a timely fashion allied with system flexibility to meet the organization's changing needs is the key deliverable for this project.

- The development of an enterprise-wide risk system is likely to impact the organizational structure and culture. The cross-functional view that is needed for this type of project may be at odds with the current organizational structure. Company politics and vested interests of the various managers may hinder or delay the implementation.

- There are likely to be some changes resulting from the implementation of the enterprise-wide risk system, both in terms of the organization and the content of some of the staff's jobs. These changes, if not managed properly, could lead to delays in the deployment of the system.

- The level of expertise, both business and technical, may not be readily available, either within the organization or the industry.

- There are likely to be substantial support and training requirements for both the technical and business staff. There may be changes to the operating procedures resulting from the requirements for an enterprise-wide risk information system.

The challenges to the implementation of the enterprise-wide risk information system are serious and quite formidable. However, there are major benefits to the organization and its staff if it can successfully implement a risk system. The enterprise-wide risk management project can have a major impact on an organization and it can be source of major change. It will impact people, processes and structure as well as the technological infrastructure. The management needs to ensure that goals are clearly defined and communicated, and that plans are in place to manage the transition and deal with organizational culture and politics.

Build or buy?

Whenever an organization needs to procure technology or systems, the decision needs to be made whether to build the system in-house or to source it from an external supplier. There are three broad options that organizations have when procuring systems:

- Develop the system in-house.

- Buy the system from an external supplier.

- Commission an external software house to develop a bespoke solution.

The decision on which strategy to adopt depends on many factors including type of system that needs to be procured, what is available on the market, the availability of technical expertise or skills in-house and the strategic importance of the system. Additionally there may be internal political issues within the technology departments that need to be addressed.

Even for individual product-based systems, where there are standard solutions available from suppliers that meet the requirements, the decision is rarely straightforward. The overhead of developing, supporting and enhancing the system in-house needs to be assessed against the cost, functionality, technology, flexibility and the level of support available from external suppliers. While procuring a system from an external supplier mitigates some of the technology risks, it does create a dependency on the supplier's ability to provide the necessary enhancements and support to reflect the organization's changing requirement.

There are a number of issues that need to be addressed when choosing which option to adopt as part of a system procurement strategy.

- The organization needs to take a clear and systematic approach with realistic expectations of functionality and timescales.

- Although I have outlined three options that are available, some of the options may not be available to you because of the corporate policy or lack of particular resources. For example, the corporate strategy may be that systems that are regarded as strategic or core cannot be procured from external suppliers.

- There needs to be a detailed statement of user requirements and functional priorities. If the company decides on the in-house option, the management need to understand additional resources that will be needed both from the business as well as technology. Some of these resources may not be readily available from within the organization. For example, having worked within a particular area does not necessarily qualify an individual to develop the specification for a new system. The analytical skills needed to develop a system requirement document are likely to be quite different from the skills required to work within an area.

- The company needs to develop a time scale for and deliverables from the project. These need to be realistic and based on the resource profile of the organization. As well as the financial resources, the organization needs to address both business and technical resource issues.

- The company needs to define the strategy for support and enhancement for the system.

- The interface requirement of the system needs to be addressed. There are still many systems available that have very limited facilities for integrating with other systems.

- Whichever option is chosen, it is important not to under-estimate the task.

Each approach has some distinct advantages and disadvantages, depending on the organization's requirements and resources.

Build or buy?

In-house development

Organizations have traditionally developed their own systems, particularly within the capital markets area. Many institutions, however, do not have the option to develop their own systems because of the timescales, lack of internal resources, or because there may be a perfectly adequate system available that meets their particular requirements. There are many reasons for opting to develop the system in house. These include lack of suitable systems; the changing nature of the markets means that systems need to be constantly enhanced; and banks relying on proprietary analytical models to manage portfolios.

Advantages

- The developments can be in line with corporate strategy for hardware platforms and software environment. The institution is able to define the requirement exactly.

- There are no conflicts with external parties in terms of development priorities. The organization only has to manage its internal priorities.

- The expertise and skills developed during the project remain within the organization.

- As organizations look to gain competitive advantage through technological innovation, any system developed in-house will be proprietary and the organization will be able to differentiate its offerings from its competitors.

Disadvantages

- The in-house development is likely to cost more than a bought-in system because of its one-off bespoke nature.

- The delivery time of the in-house development is likely to be substantially longer than the equivalent bought-in solution.

- The project is likely to be resource intensive in terms of management, business and technical resources. Definitions of user requirements, system specifications and testing are time-consuming activities that require heavy involvement from the users.

- Unless there is an adequate level of project management expertise, the company can be exposed to both technology risk and project management risk.

- The company needs to plan for the on-going support and maintenance. There is a requirement to retain specialist information technology professionals within the organization.

Before embarking on an in-house development of a system, the organization needs to ensure that it has the right type and level of resources and expertise to undertake and complete the project. It needs to understand the rationale for wanting to undertake the project in-house and ensure that provision is made for the long-term support and maintenance of the system.

Deciding to buy a system

While this is a popular option, particularly for standard product-based systems, there are a number of questions that need to answered when opting for this solution. For example:

- Are there systems available that meet your requirement and are these available from suppliers that your company would be happy doing business with?

- Does the supplier have sufficient resources and business expertise to provide the level of support that your business may require?

- Does the supplier have sufficient business and development resources to keep the product in line with market needs and to support your company's business requirements?

Build or buy?

- Are there any platform compatibility or system integration issues?

There are many reasons why an organization may choose to buy a system as opposed to building the system. The pros and cons of this approach are outlined below.

Advantages

- The cost is likely to be substantially less than the in-house development and the costs are generally known and fixed at the start of the project. The product is likely to be available immediately.

- The system is likely to be functionally very rich because of a larger customer base. Much of the standard functionality will already have been developed to meet the market and regulatory requirements. There is likely to a greater level of management reporting functionality.

- The solution is normally tried and tested. Any software errors are likely to be quickly discovered due to greater volume of testing, beta sites and larger customer base.

- The organization does not need to get involved in managing a software project with all its associated risks.

- The supplier is likely to continually upgrade the product to keep pace with the changes in market requirements, business practice and technological developments.

- The support and maintenance costs are likely to be lower than having your own team of development staff.

- With more systems available with open architecture, integration with internal systems is less of an issue.

Disadvantages

- The nature of a packaged solution is that there is likely to be limited opportunity to differentiate the product or services from other institutions using the same product.

- There is likely to be limited control over development priorities. Systems enhancements required by your business may not be available due to conflicts with other customer requirements.

- The level of support available is often a problem. All too frequently companies provide support staff who may have knowledge of the product at a technical level but have little or no idea about how to use the system in a business environment.

- The supplier's technology platform may not be compatible with your corporate strategy.

- The integration of the external systems with existing systems may be a problem.

Outsourcing the development to an external supplier

The late 1980s and 1990s have seen a tremendous growth in outsourcing activity. Organizations have outsourced many non-core activities, which has led to the development of strategic partnerships that are mutually beneficial to both organizations. Outsourcing of systems development projects to specialist software houses is an extension of that process. It allows the financial institutions to develop bespoke solutions without the overhead of having to hire and retain IT staff. If an institution has specific requirements that cannot be met by a standard solution or where the planned system is expected to provide a key competitive advantage or service differentiation and the organization does not have the development resource to undertake the project in-house, then outsourcing the development and support to a specialist organization provides an ideal solution. Companies should explore this option even when there are internal resources available.

In many instances where there is no 'off-the-shelf' solution available, this approach provides access to professional resources without the need for the organization to invest in its own IT staff. This approach has a lot of the advantages of the in-house development option.

Advantages

- The organization can specify the exact solution that is needed.

- There are no conflicts with external parties in terms of development priorities.

- Once the scope of the system has been agreed, the costs are likely to fixed and stable.

- Some of the technology risk can be devolved to the supplier through a contractual relationship.

- The organization retains control and strategic direction of the developments.

- The software development approach is likely to be more professional and structured than in-house developments.

- While the organization retains the control of the strategy and policy, it does not need to get involved in the day-to-day management of the project.

- By developing partnership agreements and strategic alliances, the organization can have access to resources that would normally not be available to it.

Disadvantages

- The project costs are likely to be greater than buying a packaged solution.

- There is greater reliance on an external supplier for key system developments that would require on-going support and enhancements.

- While the supplier would have software development and project management expertise, it is unlikely to have the detailed business knowledge or expertise. There is likely to be a substantial call on business users' time during system specification and testing.

- For strategic systems such as an enterprise-wide risk information system, confidentiality of information may be an issue.

- Unless the initial scope and specifications are carefully and comprehensively defined, there are likely to be cost and time over-runs. Later enhancements, while being essential to the project, can add appreciably to the original costs.

- There is likely to be dilution of in-house skills. The copyright for any developed software is likely to be retained by the supplier.

- If a number of projects are outsourced to a strategic partner, there is likely to be concentration of operational risk.

In adopting this approach, the organization needs to ensure the requirements are carefully defined and well understood by both parties. The responsibilities of the external partner need to be carefully defined. It is important to remember that you are buying resources for a particular project, not devolving strategic development responsibility to an external supplier.

The advantages and disadvantage of the various options for procuring information systems are outlined above. All the options may not be available to an organization due to corporate policy, system availability or supplier profile.

However, for enterprise-wide risk management, buying an existing system is not really an option for a number of reasons. First, there are no risk systems available that adequately cover and process all the products and instruments that an organization is likely to transact. Second, there is unlikely to be a system available that would interface with all of the organization's existing product- or business-based systems. Third, the existing technology infrastructure for different organizations will be different. Fourth, the enterprise-wide risk management solution depends on the organizational culture and structure. The risk system would need to fit into an overall risk appetite and risk management strategy and therefore the technology solution is likely to be different for each organization. The risk solution for each organization is likely to be a bespoke development based on system components that would already exist within the organization in support of the existing business units and additional components, either developed or bought in, to facilitate the data integration and risk oversight and reporting functionality.

For the enterprise-wide risk information system, the decision that an organization needs to make is whether to develop the system totally in house or whether to outsource the development to an external software house.

13 | Project management for an enterprise-wide risk management system

As organizations move away from functional structures, where individual specialist skills are grouped together into single departments, to project organizations, where the focus is on integrated project teams that include all the functional expertise necessary for the project, there is a requirement to adopt new management models. The project teams are responsible for introducing change in the organization, both organizational and technical, and are brought together for the duration of the project. A project can be the development and implementation of a small local system that only affects an individual or a small group or a co-ordinated set of enterprise wide activities that fundamentally change the organizational culture and mindset. Project management is an important function within the organization and is a key activity in managing operational risk within a financial institution.

The introduction of an enterprise-wide risk management system can affect the whole structure of the organization and is likely to impact all the major functional areas of the financial institution including trading, operations, information technology, communications, compliance, regulatory reporting and risk management. In order to effectively manage a project of this type and scope it is imperative that project management procedures are in place that cover the complete project life cycle including project planning, progress measurement, reporting, managing the financial aspects of the project and implementation and operation of the system. These procedures are designed to ensure that the change is delivered on time, within budget and that it meets the business needs.

Regardless of whether the risk management system is being developed in-house or procured from an external vendor, a project management framework based on the issues outlined in the following sections should be adopted.

To successfully manage and implement an enterprise-wide risk management project, a number of often conflicting needs have to be addressed. There needs to be sufficient flexibility in the overall strategy and effective monitoring and reporting to allow plans to be adequately modified to reflect changes in the project as it progresses. While a number of technology risks have been highlighted earlier in this book, the core nature of risk management systems and the technologies involved means that the project management process must explicitly address the following types of risks.

Technology risk

The nature of the enterprise-wide risk management systems means that it is likely to use many state-of-the-art technologies. This introduces additional risk in the project. There is the potential that a component or piece of software might fail or not work as expected. Additionally, the organization may not have the appropriate infrastructure or staff to support the new technology. Untried technology will increase the lead-time to a successful implementation of the project as there is likely to be additional and more comprehensive requirement for testing.

Scheduling risk

Enterprise-wide systems development is as much about data integration and consolidation as about developing new functionality. The initial identification and estimation of the tasks and their subsequent progress reporting and monitoring will ensure that there are no unexpected delays to the project. The project monitoring should track percentage completion of tasks against cost incurred as well as reviewing the estimated time remaining to complete the project.

Financial risk

Managing financial risk is one of the key activities of project management. Financial reporting and financial control are the principal methods for the management of the cost of the project and for ensuring that adequate levels of funding are available at the required time. Monitoring project spend against budgeted costs will ensure that any issues of over-spend are highlighted at the earliest opportunity.

Supplier risk

On a project of this nature there is likely to be substantial reliance on external suppliers for development, testing and integration expertise. Additionally, all the hardware is likely to be externally procured. The requirement, therefore, is to manage supplier risk as part of the project management process. Supplier risk increases particularly where a multiple vendor solution is being implemented due to the difficulty of enforcing common standards and interfaces.

Infrastructure risk

As well as external factors, there are a number of internal factors that need to be addressed as part of the project management activity, particularly in the implementation phase of the project. The issues include lack of internal infrastructure, particularly lack of adequately skilled or trained staff and inadequate procedures or tools to support the activities. In any implementation of a risk management system, there is likely to be substantial data conversion activity. The effort required for data conversion should not be underestimated and should be addressed at the earliest possible opportunity.

Business control and security risk

As economies become more sophisticated in their data management and usage and organizations move towards an era where the key source of competitive advantage is the information stored in the computer systems, there is increased risk that data manipulation and fraud, disclosure of sensitive information and destruction of databases or key applications will cause serious disruption to vital services. The use of client-server technologies and end-user developments, increased use of the Internet or intranets for financial transactions, and the outsoucing of both tactical and strategic systems further increases this risk.

The development of effective business controls and technical security measures becomes prerequisite for system development and implementation.

Project management framework

In order to manage the implementation of an enterprise-wide risk management system, the management needs to ensure that appropriate project management procedures are in place to cover the complete project life cycle. The issues that need to be addressed include procedures for project planning, progress measurement and reporting, managing the project finances and project implementation. These procedures are designed to ensure that the project is delivered on time, within budget and that it meets the needs of the business.

The framework outlined below is designed to ensure that there are adequate project management controls covering all aspects of the project and it focuses on procedures that help to ensure that the project is progressing satisfactorily and that project plans address all foreseeable tasks. It should be noted that the scope and degree of project control depends on the size and complexity of the individual projects. For smaller and less critical projects, the necessity for rigorous and detailed procedures is far less important but still requires a level of control to be maintained. For large, complex and sensitive projects, such as enterprise-wide risk management systems, where costs are significant or the business risk is potentially high, much more extensive controls are necessary in order to manage the risks.

Project manager

A project manager is an individual to whom authority, responsibility and accountability has been assigned to achieve the project objectives within defined time scale, cost and quality and performance criteria. The role of the project manager is crucial to the success of the project. The more complex the system under development, the more sophisticated the managers and management procedures need to be. The development and implementation of an enterprise-wide risk management system, where the project impact is likely to be across many functional areas, requires a competent and experienced project manager. To manage a project of this type a good project manager should have the following skills:

- previous successful project management experience;

- understanding of the technology required;

- understanding of the business and the user community;

- understanding of user requirements and expectations;

- credibility with the user community;

- planning skills;

- leadership skills;

- interpersonal skills;

- communication skills;

- team building capability;

- ability to grow with the assignment;

- systems engineering training and experience;

- decision analysis training and experience; and

- problem solving skills.

While a smaller and less demanding project management role may only require a sub-set of the above skills, for the implementation of an enterprise-wide risk management system the project manager or project management team should have all the above skills.

The project manager and his/her team need to be given responsibility and authority for all stages of the project to ensure that:

- the scope of the work remains focused on the original objectives;

- all tasks are identified and completed in a timely manner;

- the work is performed on time and to budget;

- there is adequate project reporting to all relevant parties;

- the business users are kept involved in the project; and

- any issues that arise are resolved or escalated to the appropriate management level in a timely manner.

Risk assessment

One of the key tasks after project initiation is the detailed risk assessment of the project. In an enterprise-wide risk management project that affects many functional areas within an organization, this is a key activity. The project risk assessment will allow the management to focus on high-risk issues and hence areas where problems are likely to arise. This will enable effective risk mitigation strategies to be developed at an early stage. All risk types including technical, financial, resource, security, organizational and safety should be considered and communicated to the project sponsor and business users. A qualitative risk assessments should be carried out to identify the risks and determine their probability and impact using low, medium and high measures. The project team should also use quantitative risk assessment techniques that will provide a much more accurate measure of the impact on costs, time scales and performance.

The initial risk assessment should be subject to constant reappraisal and review throughout the life of the project to ensure that it continues to reflect the relevant issues and any additional risks that may become apparent later in the project are highlighted. In addition, the effectiveness of actions taken to mitigate the risks must be periodically assessed and appropriate steps taken to address any differences.

Technical issues

In an enterprise-wide risk management project, there are a great many technical issues that need to be addressed. These issues include hardware platforms, software tools and environment to be used in the development, whether to develop in-house or outsource and whether to develop a bespoke solution or buy an off-the-shelf product. The expertise and infrastructure that is already in place often dictate some of the decisions. However, there are a great number of technical decisions that need to be made early on in the project and these will significantly affect the future direction and scope of the project. It is therefore vital that the right development platforms and development tools are selected to ensure that any solution that is developed is manageable, properly integrated into the existing infrastructure and is capable of being upgraded in the future.

The technical decisions taken will be strategic in nature. It is, therefore, very important that the project manager and his/her team have sufficiently detailed technical knowledge to ensure that the technical architecture for the system does not give rise to risks which are likely to compromise the viability of the project.

Project schedules

Project scheduling is one of the critical management tasks as it dictates the time frames in which the project will be completed, the budgets/costs in terms of resource requirement and the sequence of tasks to be completed. It is also important to consider the dependencies between tasks so that the correct start and finish points are identified within the overall project plan. There will be certain tasks on which the success of the whole project depends and these must be identified and closely monitored.

One of the most important tools in the armoury of the project manager is the work breakdown structure (WBS). This allows the projects to be decomposed into tasks, the work packages and finally activities. Building a WBS will identify all tasks and dependencies. Additionally, as tasks are identified and allocated to teams, an organizational breakdown structure (OBS) and a responsibility matrix begin to emerge for the project. This in turn will lead to initial cost estimates for the various tasks and work packages that will provide an understanding of cash-flow requirements for the project.

The two components of scheduling, namely estimation and planning, follow the WBS activity. The nature and scope of an enterprise-wide risk management system means that you can only begin to estimate once the project has been decomposed into work packages and activities. Increasingly organizations are adopting more scientific methods of estimating that are based on an objective assessment of the work to be performed and an interactive approach to refining the original estimate.

Project planning is a complex task involving the following procedures:

- Identifying of all the tasks to be performed given the scope of the project and technical and business constraints. This is the outcome of the WBS activity.

- Assigning those tasks to the available resources.

- Balancing completion dates against the available resources to complete all tasks within the available time.

- Critical path analysis to identify those tasks which are critical to the success and timely completion of the project.

- Identifying dependencies between tasks so that they are scheduled in the correct sequence.

- Identifying realistic start and end points (elapsed time) to accommodate the number of employee-days work for each given task.

The WBS activity will address all the issues described above and will help produce a hierarchical project plan with high-level generic tasks decomposed into work packages and individual activities. This structured approach results in a comprehensive plan that clearly identifies all the tasks and ensures that they are correctly sequenced.

There are various methods of presenting the plan; for example, in tabular form, Gantt charts and network diagrams (PERT charts). The advantage of the diagrammatic forms is that they facilitate the identification of the critical path and those tasks that are crucial to the success of the project. There are many software tools available that assist in project planning and monitoring.

Progress monitoring and control

Once the project is under way and the plans in place, it is necessary to monitor progress against the plans to provide early warning of potential problems and variances against budgets. The project control function can take any necessary remedial action.

There are a number of tools for monitoring the progress of the project. These tools include Gantt charts, slip charts, networks, monitoring against milestones and costs, and performance reports. It is important that monitoring procedures should be as objective as possible to provide a true reflection of the project status. One easy method of monitoring the project is to analyse the time spent to date against budgeted time for the task and time remaining to complete the task. Although this may give an indication of the progress, it does not necessarily tell the whole story. For example, if a project has consumed 70 per cent of its allocated budget, it does not necessarily follow that the actual work performed to date represents 70 per cent of the task. It is therefore necessary to monitor estimated time to completion against the remaining budgeted time. This will enable management to identify adverse variances against plans at an early stage and take appropriate remedial action.

Cost is of primary concern for any project and management of cost is a key activity for the project manager. Managing costs is much more than simply monitoring cash flow with time. Effective cost management requires a number of activities:

- Budgets to be set for individual work packages. This is done when the WBS is developed. These work packages are then monitored and an assessment is made of the percentage of the cost expanded against work completed.

- Milestone payments are another important form of cost management. As these are payments against deliverables or completed phases of work, they serve as time and cost measures of work.

External suppliers and influences

There are likely to be many external parties to the development of a risk management system. These include hardware suppliers, development tool experts, software experts, external development teams and external consultants. Furthermore, there are likely to be interfaces to and feeds from many different and disparate vendors and systems. The project can, therefore, be exposed to the risks of:

- failure to deliver on time at the right price;

- failure to deliver a product which works;

- failure to deliver a product which is integrated with the rest of the system; and

- failure to deliver a product which conforms to the original specification.

It is important for the project management team to ensure that all interfaces to third-party products are clearly defined and subject to agreed specifications. Additionally, all products must be subject to maintenance contracts and/or service level agreements.

Third-party suppliers of goods and services are not the only external influence on the progress of a project. Legal and regulatory requirements should also be taken into account. Regulatory bodies can impact the whole development through changes in regulations which affect the required functionality. The global nature of the investment-banking environment means that the risk management system may need to comply with a number of national and international regulatory and government bodies. The impact of changes in the regulatory environment must be assessed in terms of the project schedules and budgets. Costs may need to be re-evaluated and additional funding made available.

Risk assessment

Implementation and operational issues

The final stage of the development is the implementation and initial operation of the system. There are three main implementation strategies; these are incremental development and implementation, parallel running with existing systems or the 'big bang' approach where the entire system is implemented in one go. The nature of the enterprise-wide risk system is such that it is unlikely to be replacing an existing system but would run in parallel with existing product- or business-unit based risk management systems. Regardless of which implementation strategy has been selected, there are a number of other issues that must be considered. These include:

- There is likely to be a substantial effort required in populating the data warehouse with existing data. Data conversion and enhancement is likely to be an essential activity.

- User training and development of user documentation and context orientated help functionality.

- Production of operators' instructions if the new system has a batch component.

- Capacity planning to ensure that existing hardware will be able to handle the additional transaction volumes and that batch work will be completed in time for the on-line activities.

- Network communications and any additional controls that will be required to ensure the network is secure and external connections are properly authenticated.

- System management and administration procedures ensuring that there are appropriately skilled staff available and that they have the tools necessary to perform their jobs.

The key objectives of project management are to ensure that systems are delivered on time and within the originally agreed budget. Planning and monitoring progress are the two critical project management tasks and failure to expand adequate effort in this area will lead to the following potential risks:

- A failure to develop adequate plans may result in the omission of key tasks.

- Plans may not assign adequate resources to each task.

- Plans may not identify and schedule those tasks that are critical to the completion of the project.

- Failure to accurately and objectively monitor project progress will result in potential problems not being identified in a timely manner.

In addition to planning and monitoring related concerns, the organization should also be aware of the risks associated with the proposed implementation strategy and the use of technology, especially when the chosen solution is not tried and trusted.

14 | Operational risk model

An effective strategy for managing operational risk requires the organization to adopt a systematic and logical enterprise-wide approach. It requires the synthesis of staff skills and expertise, processes, organizational culture and structure, and the technological infrastructure. Like quality, risk management cannot be developed through constant inspection or control; it needs to become part of everyone's normal working practice. Managing risk needs to move on from the annual or six monthly audit activities and become a continuous process within the organization.

In today's fast moving markets effective risk management is not about organizations relying on increased controls, excessive monitoring, or strict procedures. It is about having a strategic vision,

Figure 14.1 Operational risk management model.

establishing a risk management culture, developing and training the staff, putting in place enterprise-wide information systems and having effective policies and procedures. In short, it is about establishing an environment that is conducive to effective risk management while retaining creativity and innovation. The main focus of the operational risk model above is the requirement for the management to bring together these various organizational components to form an integrated whole that will develop and evolve in line with the changing competitive environment.

The risk management model adopted depends on the resources, culture and the infrastructure of the organization. The underlying risk management framework needs to reflect the organization's risk appetite, policies and practices outlined by the management and take into account the regulatory environment and the industry best practices. The requirements are to identify, measure, monitor and manage all the risks within this consistent framework. The key aspect of any risk management framework is the ability of the senior management to communicate, through word and action, their risk appetite and tolerance to all areas of the business. This includes those responsible for the management and control of risk as well as those responsible for trading and risk taking activities. However, this communication flow from the senior management needs to be matched by the information flow upwards from all the various business and control units to ensure that an integrated risk management approach can be adopted.

The establishment of the risk management framework is an enterprise-wide activity and would include many departments and functions within the organization. These include strategic business managers, the various trading functions, risk managers, control and compliance functions, operations, information technology functions and human resource management professionals. The principle aim of the risk management framework is to ensure that there is transparency in the risk processes; that the integrated and consistent approach to risk is apparent to staff at all levels of the organization; that all risk exposures (including market, credit and operational) are identified and covered and that the responsibilities for risk control and risk management are clearly assigned. The risk management framework for an institution should meet the following broad objectives:

- Ensure that the organization identifies and understands all the risks involved in its activities and consciously identifies the risks it wants to adopt and those it wants to offload.

- Ensure that there are effective and efficient risk management processes.

- Ensure that timely and accurate information is available such that sound risk management decisions can be made.

- Ensure that the organization complies with the various government and regulatory bodies.

Operational risk management cycles

Figure 14.2 identifies the main activities in the operational risk management cycle. An effective risk management approach requires the organization to understand its risk appetite; this helps the institution to set risk management objectives and targets.

Having defined the risk management objectives, the organization needs to analyse all its processes and workflows to identify and list

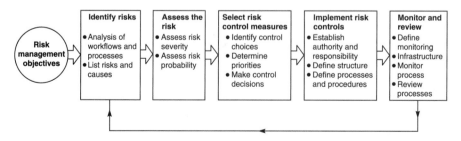

Figure 14.2 Operational risk management cycle.

the potential hazards and risks and their causes. It is important to include all processes in this initial review so that a comprehensive list of all risks and their causes is identified and recorded. Any omissions at this stage are likely to impact the rest of the cycle.

The next stage of the operational risk management cycle is the assessment of the risks. The assessment process should address the criticality/severity of the identified risks as well as the probability or frequency of particular events occurring.

Based on this information, the organization should be able to identify the various control choices that are available, assess their impact on the organization and its staff and define risk control priorities. This will allow the management to select the most appropriate risk controls for their organization and define an action plan for all the risks that have been identified.

The implementation of the risk controls should be clear and apparent to all the staff and should clearly identify where the authority, responsibility and accountability for the control process lies. As with any change there should be training and support for all staff to enable them to perform the tasks allocated to them. There should be an independent monitoring and review of the control structure so that any new or additional risk management issues are identified and addressed.

In order to manage risk, an organization needs to address two key components of the risk management process.

- *Strategic risk management* – This primarily deals with the organization's risk environment.

- *Tactical risk management and control* – This component addresses the operational procedures and the risk management control functions.

An effective risk management strategy requires a consistent

approach to both these components. A suitable strategic approach or risk environment without the necessary monitoring and control is unlikely to provide effective risk management. In the same way, excessive emphasis on controls is likely to lead to problems being hidden and thus create an even bigger risk management nightmare. It is only through an enterprise-wide approach that addresses both these components of the risk management process that an organization can truly hope to manage all the risks that it is likely to be exposed to.

Risk environment

A substantial part of the risk environment component of the risk management process is often overlooked by organizations. Whilst issues such as risk oversight, organizational structure and technological infrastructure are addressed to some extent, very little emphasis is placed on what are sometimes regarded as the soft issues of risk management such as risk appetite, staff training and empowerment, communication and organizational culture.

In the past, financial institutions may have been able to function adequately without a comprehensive approach to the risk environment. However, the financial disasters of the 1990s have shown that in the current fast moving and competitive environment such an approach can no longer work. Organizations need to develop a strategic approach that addresses the risk environment in total in order to develop a framework around which the risk management and control activities can take place. An organization's risk environment provides a number of key indicators about the seriousness of its risk management activities. In addressing the risk environment, organizations need to ensure that:

- Senior management develop a philosophy of risk awareness. They need to develop a risk aware culture and align the organization objectives and business strategy to effective risk management practices.

- The risk management and control policies need to be defined, communicated and regularly reviewed. The day-to-day risk control and management functions need to be established and must be independent of the risk taking activity. It is vital that the policies are communicated to all the staff and that there are processes to enforce these policies and standards.

- The organizational infrastructure needs to define clear lines of responsibility and authority for risk taking, risk measuring, risk monitoring and risk managing at all levels of the organization. There needs to be clear separation between risk taking, risk control and strategic risk management activities. Unambiguous and clearly defined roles will help minimize uncertainty, misunderstandings and confusion. Lack of clarity can impact the effectiveness of the organizations' control infrastructure and can lead to the types of problems faced by Barings Bank.

- Organizational charts should address both line responsibility and oversight responsibility. Any conflict of interest, inadequate checks and balances, lack of assigned responsibility or unofficial authority shown in the organizational charts should be addressed and rectified. There should be an explicit distinction between those authorized to trade and those authorized to clear trades.

- The risk management procedures and processes should reflect the operational and strategic business direction. This should include risk tolerances and limits, legal framework and documentation, approved markets and counterparties, measuring and monitoring of exposures as well as procedures for reacting to market problems and developments.

- There needs to be a strong, centralized and independent risk management and control function with an adequate level of resource and the necessary training and support to ensure that all the staff have the skills and expertise to undertake the tasks allocated to them.

- The staff appraisal, evaluation and review programmes should reflect the organization's policy toward risk management. The risk management culture of the institution should be reflected in the type and level of resources, the recruitment processes and remuneration schemes as well as staff development and training.

- The method of compensation is another way of nurturing a risk management culture. The board must adopt a compensation policy that does not encourage its risk-takers to take on unnecessary risk. For example, if the organization adopts a one-dimensional compensation policy regarding bonus payment that is based entirely on the profitability of the firm's financial transactions, it will only tempt a risk-taker. Instead, the compensation policy should additionally take into account other factors such as divisional and team performance, and the risk-taker's value-added to non-trading activities, etc.

- While there will be specific risk functions within the organization, all staff must be made aware of their responsibility for risk management. The risk taking units must be aware of the risks that they generate and bear responsibility for complying with risk policies, risk limits and risk controls.

Risk management and control functions can only work effectively in a risk aware corporate environment. While organizations may be able to demonstrate short-term gains by adopting a strict monitoring and control regime, long-term management of risk is dependent on creating a risk-aware environment and culture.

Risk management and control

While the risk environment consists primarily of corporate and cultural aspects, the control function outlines the actual policies, processes and procedures that need to be followed in order to effectively manage risk within an organization. As most of the major losses within the finance industry have been as a result of inappropriate procedures, lax monitoring, inadequate systems or unworkable management structures, the control function within the institutions has received a lot of attention during the 1990s.

The control function is a key element in the risk management process; it is not just a procedure or policy that is performed by certain individuals within specified departments at defined points in time, but rather it is something that affects all levels within an investment institution. While the senior management has a key responsibility in developing the control procedures, affective monitoring processes and an appropriate organizational culture, it is vitally important that each individual within the organization 'buys into' and participates in this process. The organizational and cultural issues have already been addressed in the previous section; this section outlines the operational control and monitoring processes that need to be in place to underpin the organization's strategic risk management vision.

The prime objectives of the control process are to ensure that:

- The performance objectives of the organizations are being achieved efficiently and effectively. The internal control process should seek to ensure that personnel throughout the organization are working to achieve the goals with efficiency and integrity, without unintended or excessive cost.

- The financial and management information is complete, reliable and is available in a timely fashion. The information received by management, the board of directors, shareholders and supervisors should be of sufficient quality and integrity that recipients can rely on the information in making decisions.

- The operation is compliant with the applicable laws and regulations. This is to ensure that all business complies with applicable laws and regulations, supervisory requirements, and the organization's policies and procedures.

Key to effective risk control is an early warning system for problems and violations. While organizational culture plays an important role, the importance of established reports and procedures to sound the alarm should not be overlooked. The management should decide in advance which policies, guidelines or limits, if violated, require exception reports, who is responsible for monitoring and reporting exceptions and to whom they must be reported. These exception guidelines should also include:

- details of any corrective actions that may be needed;

- who will have responsibility to monitor the corrective actions; and

- who is authorized to make exceptions to the exception policy.

Functional segregation is a key issue in establishing a control environment. There is the obvious segregation between the trading and the settlement functions; however, organization should also review functions such as position maintenance, treasury function, compliance, audit and risk management to ensure that there are no conflicts of interest. There should be adequate checks and balances to ensure oversight exists for each function and is independent of the area overseen. There must be clear delineation of responsibilities between front office and back office that should always be staffed and supervised separately. There must also be independent verification of position data, profit and loss figures and individual transaction details between the front and back offices.

In order to ensure effective control environment, the management must put in place the following control processes:

- The senior manager responsible for the business must understand the rationale for the institution's trading activity and they must establish guidelines and procedures for these activities that include:

- Identifying the personnel authorized to trade the various instruments and the strategies that can be used.

- Where the trading is for clients, documentation and evidence that the client accounts have given authorization for the use of the proposed instruments.

- The position or trading limits that must be applied to each trader, or client account.

- The procedures for receipt and issuance of confirmations, statements and other documentation pertaining to the trading activity.

● The monitoring of compliance with these procedures and limits should be undertaken daily or at regular intervals and should be performed by a person independent from the trading personnel. Senior management may wish to consider that at regular intervals this should incorporate an independent party.

● The management must establish, implement and monitor primary settlement policies and controls that include:

- Daily reconciliation of trades.

- Daily reconciliation of margin requirements for derivatives positions.

- Daily reconciliation of open positions.

- Monitoring of hedge or arbitrage trades to ensure all constituents are in place.

- Monitoring of delivery periods for contracts with open positions.

- Monitoring potential deliveries and location of depository

Risk management and control

instructions for any derivatives contracts going to delivery.

- Senior management should establish the procedures and policies to ensure that there is adequate segregation of personnel within the back office. There should be procedures to monitor that this segregation is being strictly complied with. Additionally, in order to minimize risk there should be routine rotation of personnel within the operations area. Management should consider a periodic independent review of the key processes within the operations area. There should be segregation between the following functions in the operations area:

  - trade processing

  - position management

  - treasury or collateral management

  - risk management

  - management reporting.

- There should be an independent review process to ensure compliance with defined procedures.

- There should be on-going and independent monitoring mechanisms for credit exposure, position limits and level of trading activities.

- Management must establish policies and procedures for the administration of excess funds and property of either the company or its clients held at counterparties.

- Directors and senior management should be fully aware of the concentration of risk when centralizing custody and clearing functions. In this type of centralized arrangement, it is important to review the performance of counterparties on a regular basis.

- Senior management must establish policies and procedures to ensure that the technology used provides the means to accurately record trades, positions, margin requirements, cash movements and any other information necessary for the complete record of all the business.

- Senior management must compile a business continuity plan. Back-up and recovery plans are crucial, as physical disasters such as the City of London bombing, the World Trade Centre bombing, the Chicago flood, the California earthquakes and hurricanes in the south eastern US made clear. Financial interruptions such as market trading halts or technological disasters such as systems, communications and power failures or software viruses also have proven the need for back-up and disaster recovery plans. A business continuity plan should include access to duplicate records of investment inventory, legal title to positions, master counterparty agreements, authorities and scheduled cash inflows and payments. It should prepare the organization to resume operations off-site in a reasonable amount of time if the primary location shuts down and should include access to contingency financing in case of a liquidity crisis.

The key to effective risk management on an enterprise-wide basis is the ability of an organization to address the strategic risk management issues and establish the tactical risk control and monitoring processes and procedures. It is only when these two components of risk management are working in harmony that the organization will be able to react effectively to the changing environment and hope to manage all the risks to which it is likely to be exposed.

15 | Conclusions

Effective risk management is crucial to the survival of an institution in rapidly moving financial markets. Derivatives have become an indispensable tool for managing and transferring the traditional market and credit risks. Whist derivatives do not create any new types of risks, the leveraged nature of the products that makes them so cost-effective when covering existing exposures, means that the effects of the market movements can be magnified both in terms of profits and losses. It therefore becomes imperative that the management understands the nature of the exposure and has effective operational controls in place to effectively monitor it.

The spectrum of risks outlined in this book include market risk (i.e. risk due to the movements in the market having an adverse effect on the portfolio), credit risk (i.e. risk that a counterparty will fail to perform on a financial obligation), and operational risk. Operational risk has been defined in its broadest sense as including organizational structure and culture, corporate strategy, people, processes, systems and controls. This inclusive nature of operational risk means that market and credit risks can only be managed effectively if the required infrastructure, including technology and business expertise, is in place.

At its broadest, operational risk can be defined as everything that is not market or credit risk. However, effective management of market and credit risks relies on systems, controls and people – all of which are components of operational risk. In looking at operational risk, the management need to consider the risk that losses will be incurred as a result of inappropriate management structure or culture, inadequate systems and internal controls, legal or regulatory issues, inadequate disaster or contingency planning, human error, or management failure.

Entering into complex financial transactions without adequate systems for measuring, monitoring, and controlling market or credit risk is an example of operational risk. An aspect of operational risk that has received significant attention in the recent years is the internal controls and oversight process. A failure at any point in the risk management chain constitutes operational risk and can result in significant losses. Many of the major financial disasters over the last few years (e.g. the collapse of Barings, losses at Sumitomo, Daiwa etc.) have not been examples straight market or credit risk. They are all examples of a lack of procedures, systems or managerial control, that is to say they are all issues associated with operational risk.

While there are many cultural and structural differences between institutions, research has shown that the operational structure within investment banks is still predominately rather bureaucratic with work being co-ordinated from the top and individuals having little input in the type or scope of their daily activities. There is still a substantial amount of manual clerical activity within the back office. Despite tremendous advances in technology, the majority of the core back office or operational systems within investment banks still rely on 1980s technology. The staff within operations tend to be young and inexperienced with limited knowledge of the business or technology. All these issues perpetuate the current operations paradigm and this has made it difficult to define a new role for the operations function within a modern financial institution.

In order to effectively manage operational risk, there needs to be a paradigm shift in the role of the operations department or the back office. Risk management is not something that can be imposed on an organization but it needs to be 'embedded' into the culture. Investment banks, particularly within the operations departments, need to move away from a bureaucratic culture to a more people-based culture. The nature of a bureaucratic culture is that while it provides the cohesion that an organization needs, it leaves very little room for the competition and conflict that are also necessary in organizations.

The central nature of the operations, both in terms of data flows and external and internal interfaces, means that it has a substantially bigger role to play in effectively managing risk within a financial institution. With flatter organizational structures, greater emphasis on staff development and training, and a more risk-aware culture, operations professionals can become much more crucial to the enterprise-wide risk management process. Greater use of technology and straight through processing will remove the need for a lot of clerical activities, leaving operations to develop more of an information and knowledge management role within the organization.

Implementation of the techniques outlined in this book will create a flexible organization, with an empowered workforce and a people-based culture that is focused on customer service. The investment in technology and communications infrastructure will allow it to capture, use and distribute information efficiently and in a timely fashion. Controls and procedures can be embedded in the technology infrastructure in the form of business rules that can be updated or amended as the business environment or market requirements change. The use of management information and decision support systems will allow management to effectively monitor the business. A risk-aware culture will ensue that risk management is the responsibility of the staff at all levels of the organization.

The key to managing operational risk is for the management to bring together the organizational structure and culture, its people and process as well as its technological infrastructure into a cohesive unit.

While technology risk is a component of operational risk, its role is crucial to the development of the organization as well as managing risk on an enterprise-wide basis. It is through the use of technology for BPR, transaction processing as well as knowledge management that those financial institutions will move toward operational excellence. The technology framework outlined in this book for enterprise-wide risk management allows organizations to monitor and manage risk more effectively and allows management to react quickly to the changing customer requirements and market movements.

Glossary

Agency relationship

A contractual relationship in which one party, the agent, acts on behalf of another party, the principal. The agent may execute trades for the principal but is not responsible for performance by the principal.

Allocation

The process of moving the trade from the executing broker to the clearing broker.

American style option

The holder of the long position can choose to exercise the position into the underlying instrument until the expiry day.

Arbitrage

A transaction in which an investor holds a basket of financial contracts which cost nothing to hold, involve no risk and result in a profit. An arbitrage transaction is based on the observation that an instrument trades at two different prices. The transaction involves selling the high-priced asset and buying the low-priced asset.

Arbitrageur

An individual who engages in arbitrage transactions.

Asset allocation

The use of derivatives by a fund manager to immediately gain or reduce exposure to different markets.

Assignment

The process by which the holder of a short option position is matched against a holder of a similar long option position who has exercised his right.

At-the-money

An option whose exercise price is equal, or very close to, the current market price of the underlying share. This option has no intrinsic value.

Automated pit system (APT)

The automated trading system used by LIFFE outside regular market hours.

Back office

The part of a firm that is responsible for post-trade activities. Depending upon the organizational structure of the firm, the back office can be a single department or multiple units (such as documentation, risk management, accounting or settlements). Some firms have combined a portion of these responsibilities, usually found in the back office, particularly those related to risk management, into what they term a middle office function. *See* Front office.

Basis risk

The risk of changes in the basis, that is, the difference between the price of a futures or forward contract and the price of the underlying asset.

Basis swap

An interest rate swap where the interest payments that are exchanged between each party are different types of floating rates.

Beta

A measure of the responsiveness of the return (or price) of a security to changes in a broader market index.

Bid price

The price at which a trader or market maker is willing to buy an instrument.

Black–Scholes option pricing model

A mathematical model developed in a seminal paper by Myron Scholes and Fisher Black in 1973. The model explains the prices on European options. Many variations of the model have been developed over the years.

Broker

A firm that communicates bid and ask levels to potential principals and otherwise arranges transactions as agent for a fee, without acting as counterparty in the transactions.

Call option

A option that gives the buyer the right but not the obligation to buy a specified quantity of the underlying instrument at a fixed price on or before a specified date. The seller of a call option has the obligation (because they have sold the right) to deliver the underlying instrument if the option is exercised by the buyer.

Cash clearing

A method for clearing futures contracts in which positions are periodically marked to market and the resulting obligations are satisfied by cash payments, known as variation margin.

CFTC

The Commodities and Futures Commission (United States).

Clearing

The centralized process whereby transacted business is recorded and positions are maintained.

Clearing house

A department of an exchange or a separate legal entity that provides a range of services related to the clearance and settlement of trades on the exchange and the management of risks associated with the resulting contracts. A clearing house is often the central counterparty to all trades on the exchange, that is, the buyer to every seller and the seller to every buyer.

Clearing link

An arrangement in which the same contract is traded on exchanges affiliated with two clearing houses but all positions are transferred daily to a single clearing house where they are carried until expiration or offset.

Clearing member

A member of a clearing house. All trades must be settled through a clearing member. A direct clearing member is able to settle only its own obligations. A general clearing member is able to settle its own obligations as well as those of clients. Variations of these two types of clearing member may also exist.

Clearing organization

The clearing organization acts as the guarantor of the performance and settlement of contracts that are traded on an exchange.

Client

A party that is not a member of the clearing house and must settle through a clearing member. Also known as customer.

Close-out

The process of offsetting existing contracts. To prevent further losses from positions carried by an entity that has defaulted, the clearing house may use close-out.

Closing trade

A bought or sold trade that is used to partly offset an open position, to reduce it or to fully offset it and close it.

Collateral

An asset that is delivered by the collateral provider to secure an obligation to the collateral taker. Collateral arrangements may take different legal forms; collateral may be obtained using the method of title transfer or pledge. Typically, government securities and cash are used as collateral in the context of OTC derivatives transactions.

Collateral management service

A centralized service that may handle any of a variety of collateral-related functions for a client firm, including valuation of collateral, confirmation of valuations with counterparties, optimization of collateral usage, and transfer of collateral.

Commodity futures

These comprise five main categories: agricultural (e.g. wheat and potatoes), softs (e.g. coffee and cocoa), precious metals (e.g. gold and silver), non-ferrous metals (e.g. copper and lead), and energies (e.g. oil and gas).

Confirm

An agreement for each individual OTC transaction which has specific terms.

Confirmation process

The procedure for verifying trade details with the counterparty. This is generally done by exchanging via fax or mail a document (i.e. a confirmation) identifying the trade details and any governing legal documentation and verifying the accuracy of the information provided by the counterparty (i.e. matching).

Contract

The standard unit of trading for futures and options. It is also commonly referred to as a 'lot'.

Contract month

The month in which futures contracts may be implemented by making or accepting delivery.

Convergence

The move to equality of spot and futures prices as the delivery date approaches.

Counterparty risk

The exposure of one party to the risk that a trade might default or fail due to the actions of the other party to the transaction.

Covered writing

The sale of call options, but the seller owns the stock which would be required to cover the delivery, if called.

Credit risk

The risk that a counterparty (such as a clearing member) will not settle an obligation for full value, either when due or at any time thereafter. Credit risk includes replacement cost risk and principal risk.

Cross currency interest rate swap

An interest rate swap where the interest payments are in two different currencies and the exchange rate, for the final settlement, is agreed at the outset of the transaction.

Currency futures

Contracts calling for delivery of a specific amount of a foreign currency at a specified future date in return for a given amount of, say, US dollars.

Currency swap

An agreement to exchange interest related payments in the same currency from fixed rate into floating rate (or vice versa) or from one type of floating rate to another. A currency swap is different to an interest rate swap as the principal amounts are also swapped.

Current exposure

The loss that would be incurred today on a contract or set of contracts if a counterparty failed to perform on its obligations. Also known as replacement cost, current exposure is what it would cost to replace a given contract if the counterparty defaulted now.

Custody risk

The risk of loss of securities held in custody occasioned by the insolvency, negligence or fraudulent action of the custodian or of a sub-custodian.

Daily settlement

The process in a futures market in which the daily price changes are paid by the parties incurring losses to the parties making profits. The profits and losses are generally settled with a clearing corporation.

Day order

An order to purchase or sell a financial claim that is cancelled if unfilled by the end of the day.

Day trader

A trader who closes out all positions by the end of the trading session.

Dealer

A firm that enters into transactions as a counterparty on both sides of the market in one or more products. OTC derivatives dealers are primarily large international financial institutions – mostly commercial banks but also some securities firms and insurance companies – as well as a few affiliates of what are primarily non-financial firms.

Default

Failure to satisfy an obligation on time. More generally, a clearing house may declare a member in default in a variety of circumstances, including failure to satisfy obligations on time, insolvency, suspension of trading privileges on an exchange for which the clearing house provides services, or other events that the clearing house deems to have had a material adverse effect on the member's capacity to meet its obligations.

Delivery

The process in which a futures contract can be terminated at the expiration of the contract through the sales of the asset by the short to the long.

Delivery notice

The written notice given by a seller indicating his intention to make delivery against an open contract.

Delivery price

The price fixed by the clearing house at which deliveries on futures contracts are invoiced.

Delivery versus payment

A link between a securities transfer system and a funds transfer system that ensures that delivery occurs if, and only if, payment occurs.

Delta

The mathematical relationship between the change in value of a call option on a bond and the change in market price of the underlying bond. Delta increases as the value of the market price of the bond rises relative to the strike price of the option. An out-of-the-money option has a delta near zero, while a significantly in-the-money option has a delta near one.

Derivative

(1) A financial contract the value of which depends on the value of one or more underlying reference assets, rates or indices. For analytical purposes, all derivatives contracts can be divided into basic building-blocks of forward contracts, options or combinations thereof. Futures, swaps, some forwards, options, warrants, and certain mortgage-backed securities are the most common derivatives.

(2) A financial instrument the value which is dependent upon the value of an underlying asset.

End-user

An entity that takes positions for investment or hedging purposes. An end-user often deals only on one side of the market. End-users include banks, insurance companies, pension funds, other financial institutions, non-financial corporations, governments, supranational entities (for example, the World Bank) and high-net-worth individuals.

Equity

A common term to describe stocks or shares.

Equity/stock options

Contracts based on individual equities or shares. On exercise of the option the specified amount of shares are exchanged between the buyer and the seller through the clearing organization.

Equity index swap

An obligation between two parties to exchange cash flows based on the percentage change in one or more stock indices, for a specific period with previously agreed re-set dates. The swap is cash settled and based on notional principal amounts. One side of an equity swap can involve a LIBOR reference rate.

ETD

This is the common term that is used to describe exchange traded derivatives, which are standardized products. It also differentiates products that are listed on an exchange as opposed to those offered over-the-counter.

European style option

An option which can only be exercised on the expiry day.

Exchange delivery settlement price (EDSP)

The price determined by the exchange for physical delivery of the underlying instrument or cash settlement.

Exchange member

A member of an exchange with certain trading privileges. An exchange member may not necessarily be a member of the exchange's clearing house.

Exchange owned clearing organization

Exchange- or member-owned clearing organizations are structured so that the clearing members guarantee each other with the use of a members' default fund and additional funding like insurance, with no independent guarantee.

Exchange-traded derivative

A derivative which is listed and traded at an organized marketplace. Derivatives exchanges generally provide standardized contracts and central clearing facilities for participants.

Execution

The action of trading in the markets.

Execution and clearing agreement

An agreement signed between the client and the clearing broker. This agreement sets out the terms by which the clearing broker will conduct business with the client.

Execution only or give-up agreement

Tripartite agreements which are signed by the executing broker, the clearing broker and the client. This agreement sets out the terms by which the clearing broker will accept business on behalf of the client.

Exercise

The process by which the holder of an option may take up their right to buy or sell the underlying asset.

Exercise price (or strike price)

The fixed price, per share or unit, at which an option conveys the right to call (purchase) or put (sell) the underlying shares or units.

Expiration

A date after which an option or futures contract is no longer in effect.

Expiry date

The last date on which an option holder can exercise their right. After this date an option is deemed to have lapsed or been abandoned.

Fair value

The value of an option derived from an option-pricing model.

Financial futures/options contracts

Financial futures is a term used to describe futures contracts based on financial instruments like currencies, debt instruments and financial indices.

First notice day

The first day that the holders of short positions can give notification to the exchange/clearing house that they wish to effect delivery.

Flat position

A position that has been fully closed out and where there is no liability to make or take delivery.

Flex options

Newly introduced contracts that are a cross between OTCs and exchange traded products. The advantage of flex options is that participants can choose various parts of the contract specification such as the expiry date and exercise price.

Floorbrokerage

The process of delegating the execution to another counterparty.

Forward (implied) rate

The rate agreed upon in a forward contract for a loan or implied by the relationship between short and long-term rates.

Forward contract

A contract in which one party agrees to buy, and the other to sell, a specified product at a specified price on a specified date or dates in the future.

Forward rate agreements

An agreement where the client can fix the rate of interest that will be applied to a notional loan or deposit, drawn or placed on an agreed date in the future, for a specified term.

Front office

A firm's trading unit and other areas that are responsible for developing and managing relationships with counterparties.

Futures

An agreement to buy or sell an asset at a certain time in the future for a certain price. Futures are traded on organized exchanges.

Futures-style margining

A method of margining derivatives contracts in which positions are marked to market and current exposures are extinguished through cash payments known as variation margin. When options contracts are margined using a futures-style system, the option premium is gradually paid over the life of the option (through the cumulative variation margin payments) and fully paid once the option has been exercised.

Gamma

The rate at which the delta of an option moves up or down in response to changes in the price of the underlying. Gamma is positive for calls and negative for puts.

Gearing

The characteristic of derivatives which enables a far greater reward for the same, or much smaller, initial outlay. It is the ratio of exposure to investment outlay.

Give-up

The process of giving a trade to a third party who will undertake the clearing and settlement of the trade.

Global clearing

The channelling of the settlement of all futures and options trades through a single counterparty or through a number of counterparties geographically located.

GLOBEX

The overnight trading system operated by Reuters and the Chicago Mercantile Exchange (CME).

Good-till-cancelled order

An order that is in effect until cancelled as is used most often with stop orders and limit orders that may take time to execute.

Gross position

A position that is held with both the bought and sold trades kept open.

Gross margining

A margining system in which the clearing member is required to deposit with the clearinghouse sufficient initial margin to cover the gross positions of its clients.

Haircut

The difference between the market value of a security and its collateral value. The haircut is intended to protect a lender of funds or securities from losses owing to declines in collateral values.

Hedging

A trading method which is designed to reduce or mitigate risk.

Holder

A person who has bought an open derivatives contract.

IMRO

The Investment Management Regulatory Organization (United Kingdom).

Independent clearing organization

The independent organization is quite separate from the actual members of the exchange, and will guarantee to each member the performance of the contracts by having them registered in the organization's name.

Initial margin

The deposit which the clearing house calls as protection against a default of a contract. It is returnable to the clearing member once the position is closed. The level is subject to changes in line with market conditions.

Interest rate futures

These are based on a debt instrument such as a government bond or a treasury bill as the underlying product and require the delivery of a bond or bill to fulfil the contract.

Interest rate swap

An agreement to exchange interest related payments in the same currency from fixed rate into floating rate (or vice versa) or from one type of floating rate to another.

In-the-money

A call option where the exercise price is below the underlying share price or a put option where the exercise price is above the underlying share price.

Intra-day margin

An extra margin call that the clearing organization can call during the day when there is a very large movement up or down in the price of the contract.

Intrinsic value

>The amount by which an option is in-the-money.

Last notice day

>The final day that notification of delivery will be possible. On most exchanges all outstanding short futures contracts will be automatically delivered to open long positions.

Last trading day

>Often the day preceding last notice day which is the final opportunity for holders of long positions to trade out of their positions and avoid ultimate delivery.

Legal risk

>The risk of loss because of the unexpected application of a law or regulation or because a contract cannot be enforced.

LIBOR

>The London inter-bank offered rate. It is the rate used when one bank borrows from another bank. It is the benchmark used to price many capital market and derivative transactions.

Liquidity risk

>The risk that a counterparty (such as a clearing member) will not settle an obligation for full value when due. Liquidity risk does not imply that a clearing member is insolvent since it may be able to settle its obligations at some unspecified time thereafter.

Local

>An individual member of an exchange who trades solely for their own account.

Long

>A position in the cash or derivatives market in which the investor owns or has contracted to own the underlying.

Lot

>The common term used to describe the standard unit of trading for futures and options. It is also referred to as a 'contract'.

Margin call

>A request from a broker or clearing house for additional funds to cover losses on an outstanding futures position.

Market counterparty

A person dealing as agent or principal with the broker and involved in the same nature of investment business as the broker.

Market maker

A trader who works for an organization such as an investment bank. They quote bids and offers in the market and are normally under an obligation to make a price in a certain number of contracts. They create liquidity in the contract by offering to buy or sell.

Market risk

The risk of losses in on- and off-balance-sheet positions arising from movements in market prices.

Market value (replacement value)

The cost that would be incurred or the gain that would be realized if an outstanding contract were replaced at current market prices.

Mark-to-market

The process of revaluing an OTC or exchange traded product each day. It is the difference between the closing price on the previous day against the current closing price. For exchange traded products this is referred to as variation margin.

Master agreement

This agreement is for OTC transactions and is signed between the client and the broker. It covers the basic terms under which the client and broker wish to transact business.

MOF

The Ministry of Finance (Japan).

Multilateral netting

Netting on a multilateral basis is arithmetically achieved by summing each participant's bilateral net positions with the other participants to arrive at a multilateral net position. Such netting is conducted through a central counterparty (such as a clearing house) that is legally substituted as the buyer to every seller and the seller to every buyer. The multilateral net position represents the bilateral net position between each participant and the central counterparty.

Mutual offset system

A link between clearing houses in which positions entered into on one exchange can be, but need not be, transferred to the clearing house of another exchange and vice versa.

Naked writing

Where the seller does not own the stock corresponding to the call option which he has sold and would be forced to pay the prevailing market price for the stock to meet delivery obligations, if called.

Net margining

A margining system in which the clearing member is required to deposit with the clearing house sufficient initial margin to cover the net positions of its clients. Clients, however, are typically still obligated to deposit with the clearing member initial margin to cover their own positions.

Netting

An offsetting of positions or obligations by counterparties.

Non clearing member

A member of an exchange who does not undertake to settle their derivatives business. This type of member must appoint a clearing member to register all their trades at the clearing organzation.

Novation

The process where registered trades are cancelled with the clearing members and substituted by two new ones – one between the clearing house and the clearing member seller, the other between the clearing house and the clearing member buyer.

Offer price

The price at which a trader or market maker is willing to sell a contract.

Offsetting order

A futures or option transaction that is the exact opposite of a previously established long or short position.

Omnibus account

A single account for containing funds or positions of multiple parties. A clearing member will often maintain an omnibus account at the clearing house for all of its clients. In this case, the clearing member is responsible for maintaining account records for individual clients.

Open interest

The number of futures or options contracts that have been established that have not yet been offset or exercised.

Open outcry

The style of trading whereby traders face each other in a designated area such as a pit and shout or call their respective bids and offers. Hand signals are also used to communicate. It is governed by exchange rules.

Open position

The number of contracts which have not been offset at the clearing organization by the close of business.

Opening trade

A bought or sold trade which is held open to create a position.

Operational risk

The risk of human error or a breakdown of some component of the hardware, software or communications systems that are critical to settlement.

Option

An option is, in the case of the buyer, the right, but not the obligation, to take (call) or make (put) for delivery of the underlying product and, in the case of the seller, the obligation to make or take delivery of the underlying product.

Option contract

A contract that gives the buyer the right, but not the obligation, to either buy or sell an underlying asset, depending on the type of option, by a certain date for a certain price. For this right, the buyer pays the seller a 'premium'.

Option premium

The sum of money paid by the buyer for acquiring the right of the option. It is the sum of money received by the seller for incurring the obligation, having sold the rights of the option. It is the sum of the intrinsic value and the time value.

Options on futures

These have the same characteristics as an option, the difference being that the underlying product is either a long or short futures contract. Premium is not exchanged as the contracts are marked to market each day.

Options-style margining

A method of margining derivatives contracts in which positions are marked to market and current exposures are collateralized. When an option contract is margined using such a system, the buyer of the option pays the premium in full at the time of the purchase. The seller of the option receives the premium and collateralizes current exposures as they occur.

Out-of-the-money

A call option whose exercise price is above the current underlying share price or a put option whose exercise price is below the current underlying share price. This option has no intrinsic value.

Out-trade

A trade which has been incorrectly matched on the floor of an exchange.

Over-the-counter (OTC)

A method of trading that does not involve an exchange. In over-the-counter markets, participants trade directly with each other, where the specifications of the product are completely flexible and non-standardized.

Payment netting

Settling payments due on the same date and in the same currency on a net basis.

Performance bond

A good-faith deposit (type of margin) to ensure performance of financial obligations in futures contracts and short options contracts on regulated commodity exchanges. Established and monitored in organized exchanges by a clearing house.

PIA

The Personal Investment Authority (United Kingdom)

Pit

The designated area on the market floor where a particular contract is traded. It may be termed a ring in some markets, e.g. LME.

Plain vanilla transactions

The most common and generally the simplest types of derivatives transaction. Plain vanilla is a relative concept, and no precise list of plain vanilla transactions exists. Transactions that have unusual or less common features are often called exotic or structured.

Position limit

A restriction on the number of contracts or share of a contract's open interest that a single entity may hold.

Potential future exposure

The additional exposure that a counterparty might potentially assume during the life of a contract or set of contracts beyond the current replacement cost of the contract or set of contracts.

Pre-settlement risk

The risk that a counterparty to an outstanding transaction for completion at a future date will fail to perform on the contract or agreement during the life of the transaction. The resulting exposure is the cost of replacing the original transaction at current market prices.

Principal risk

The risk that the seller of a security delivers a security but does not receive payment or that the buyer of a security makes payment but does not receive delivery. In this event, the full principal value of the securities or funds transferred is at risk.

Principal-to-principal market

A market where the clearing house only recognizes the clearing member as one entity, and not the underlying clients of the clearing member.

Principal-to-principal relationship

A contractual relationship in which both parties are acting on their own behalf and are responsible for the performance of any contractual obligations.

Private customer

> An individual person who is not acting in the course of carrying on investment business.

Proprietary trader

> A trader who deals for an organization such as an investment bank taking advantage of short-term price movements as well as taking long-term views on whether the market will move up or down.

Put option

> An option that gives the buyer the right, but not the obligation, to sell a specified quantity of the underlying asset at a fixed price, on or before a specified date. The seller of a put option has the obligation (because they have sold the right) to take delivery of the underlying asset if the option is exercised by the buyer.

RCH

> Recognised Clearing House under the Financial Services Act (SIB).

Real-time gross settlement (RTGS)

> The continuous settlement of funds or securities transfers individually on an order-by-order basis.

Replacement cost risk

> The risk that a counterparty to an outstanding transaction for completion at a future date will fail to perform on the settlement date. The resulting exposure is the cost of replacing, at current market prices, the original transaction.

RIE

> Recognised Investment Exchange under the Financial Services Act (SIB)

Ring

> The designated area on the market floor where a particular contract is traded. It may be termed a pit in some markets, e.g. CBOT.

Screen-based trading

> A method of trading which takes place by the dealers inputting their bids and offers into screens linked to a computer system. There is no exchange floor and the traders operate the computer screens from their own offices.

Seats

The term given to describe the membership of an exchange that entitles the holder to execute business on the exchange and in certain cases carries voting rights. A seat must be held in order to be a member of an exchange and they can be purchased from the exchange or can be leased from other member firms, depending upon availability.

SEC

The Securities and Exchange Commission (United States).

Segregation

A method of protecting client assets and positions by holding or accounting for them separately from those of the carrying firm or broker.

Segregation of funds

Where the client assets are held separately from those assets belonging to the member firm.

Series

All options of a given class with the same exercise price and expiration date.

Settlement

The fulfilment of the contractual commitments of transacted business.

Settlement bank

Either a central bank or a private bank used to effect money settlements.

Settlement price

The official price established by the clearing house at the end of each day for use in the daily settlement.

Settlement risk

The risk that the seller of a security or funds delivers its obligation but does not receive payment or that the buyer of a security or funds makes payment but does not receive delivery. In this event, the full principal value of the securities or funds transferred is at risk.

Share futures

These are based on individual shares. Delivery is fulfilled by the payment or receipt of cash against the exchange calculated delivery settlement price.

Short

A sold position in a derivative which is held open.

SIB

The Securities and Investments Board (United Kingdom), appointed by HM Treasury to oversee the three self-regulatory organizations.

Single-currency interest rate swap

An interest rate swap where the interest payments are exchanged in the same currency.

SPAN

Standardized portfolio analysis of risk. A form of margin calculation which is used by various clearing organizations.

Speculator

A person who buys or sells contracts in the hope of profiting from subsequent price changes.

SRO

Self Regulatory Organization under the Financial Services Act (SFA, IMRO, PIA).

Stock index futures/options

Based on the value of an underlying stock index like the FTSE 100 in the UK, the S&P 500 index in the USA and the Nikkei 225 and 300 in Japan. Delivery is fulfilled by the payment or receipt of cash against the exchange-calculated delivery settlement price. They are referred to as both indices and indexes.

Straddle

An option transaction that involves a long position in a put and a call and with the same exercise price and expiration.

Straight-through processing

The capture of trade details directly from front-end trading systems and complete automated processing of confirmations and settlement instructions without the need for rekeying or reformatting data.

Strangle

A long put at one exercise price and a long call at a higher exercise price.

Stress testing

The estimation of credit and liquidity exposures that would result from the realization of extreme price changes.

Strike price

Exercise price.

Swaps

A forward contractual agreement to exchange one type of cash flow or asset for another, according to predetermined rules. An interest rate swap is a contract between two counterparties to exchange fixed-interest payments for floating-interest payments. An equity index swap might involve swapping the returns on two different stock market indexes or swapping the index return for an interest rate such as LIBOR. A currency swap might involve exchanging two currencies and the interest payments required to borrow the funds in the respective countries issuing the currencies.

Systemic risk

The risk that the failure of one participant in a payment or settlement system, or in financial markets generally, to meet its required obligations when due will cause other participants or financial institutions to be unable to meet their obligations (including settlement obligations in a transfer system) when due. Such a failure may cause significant liquidity or credit problems and, as a result, might threaten the stability of financial markets.

Theta

The rate at which the price of an option changes because of the passage of time. This is also known as time decay.

Tick

The minimum permissible price fluctuation established by an organized market.

Time value

The amount by which an option's premium exceeds its intrinsic value. Where an option has no intrinsic value the premium consists entirely of time value.

Trade matching

The process of matching trade details (such as number of contracts, contract month and price) submitted by the trade counterparties. The clearing-house often guarantees a trade at the time it is successfully matched.

Trade registration

The process by which matched trades are formally recorded on the books of the clearing house. For clearing houses that act as central counterparties, registration may also be the time at which the clearing house substitutes itself as counterparty to the clearing members.

Traded option

An option which is traded on an exchange.

Trading permits

These are issued by exchanges and give the holder the right to have one trader at any one time trading in the contract(s) to which the permit relates.

Underlying

The asset on which a futures or option is written.

Value at risk

An estimate of the upper bound on losses an institution would expect to incur during a given period (for example, one day) for a given confidence level (for example, 95 per cent).

Variation margin

The process of revaluing an exchange-traded product each day. It is the difference between the closing price on the previous day and the current closing price. It is physically paid or received each day by the clearing organization. It is often referred to as the mark-to-market.

Warrant

A security convertible into a specified number of shares of stock, a call option.

Writer

A person who has sold an open derivatives contract and is obliged to deliver or take delivery upon notification of exercise from the buyer.

Appendix 1 | Exchange codes

AEX – Amsterdam Exchange
AMEX – American Stock Exchange
ASXD – Australian Stock Exchange Derivatives
BCE – Budapest Commodities Exchange
BM&F – Bolsa de Mercadorias & Futuros
CBOE – Chicago Board of Options Exchange
CBOT – Chicago Board of Trade Exchange
CME – Chicago Mercantile Exchange
COMEX – New York Mercantile Exchange
CSCE – Coffee, Sugar and Cocoa Exchange
Eurex D – Eurex Deutschland
HKFE – Hong Kong Futures Exchange
IPE – International Petroleum Exchange
LIFFE – London International Financial Futures Exchange
LME – London Metal Exchange
MATIF – Marche a Terme International de France
MEFF RF – Meff Renta Fija
MEFF RV – Meff Renta Variable
MICEX – Moscow Interbank Currency Exchange
NYMEX – New York Mercantile Exchange
OM – Stockholm Options Market
OSE – Osaka Securities Exchange
PHLX – Philadelphia Stock Exchange
SAFEX – South African Stock Exchange
SFE – Sydney Futures Exchange
SIMEX – Singapore International Monetary Exchange
TGE – Tokyo Grain Exchange
TIFFE – Tokyo International Financial Futures Exchange
TOCOM – Tokyo Commodities Exchange
TSE – Tokyo Stock Exchange

Appendix 2 | Operational risk management[1]

The Basle Committee on Banking Supervision has recently initiated work related to operational risk. Managing such risk is becoming an important feature of sound risk management practice in modern financial markets. The most important types of operational risk involve breakdowns in internal controls and corporate governance. Such breakdowns can lead to financial losses through error, fraud, or failure to perform in a timely manner or cause the interests of the bank to be compromised in some other way, for example, by its dealers, lending officers or other staff exceeding their authority or conducting business in an unethical or risky manner. Other aspects of operational risk include major failure of information technology systems or events such as major fires or other disasters.

A working group of the Basle Committee recently interviewed approximately thirty major banks from the different member countries on the management of operational risk. Several common themes emerged during these discussions:

- Awareness of operational risk among bank boards and senior management is increasing. Virtually all banks assign primary responsibility for managing operational risk to the business line head. Those banks that are developing measurement systems for operational risk often are also attempting to build some form of incentive for sound operational risk management practice by business managers. This incentive could take the form of a capital allocation for operational risk, inclusion of operational risk measurement into the performance evaluation process, or requiring business line management to present operational loss details and resultant corrective action directly to the bank's highest levels of management.

● While all banks surveyed have some framework for managing operational risk, many banks indicated that they were only in the early stages of developing an operational risk measurement and monitoring framework. Awareness of operational risk as a separate risk category has been relatively recent in most of the banks surveyed. Few banks currently measure and report this risk on a regular basis, although many track operational performance indicators, analyse loss experiences and monitor audit and supervisory ratings.

● Many banks have identified significant conceptual issues and data needs, which would need to be addressed in order to develop general measures of operational risk. Unlike market and perhaps credit risk, the risk factors are largely internal to the bank and a clear mathematical or statistical link between individual risk factors and the likelihood and size of operational loss does not exist. Experience with large losses is infrequent and many banks lack a time series of historical data on their own operational losses and their causes. While the industry is far from converging on a set of standard models, such as are increasingly available for market and credit risk measurement, the banks that have developed or are developing models rely on a surprisingly similar set of risk factors. Those factors include internal audit ratings or internal control self-assessments, operational indicators such as volume, turnover or rate of errors, loss experience, and income volatility.

Additional details from the interviews are discussed below under five categories: management oversight; risk measurement, monitoring and management information systems; policies and procedures; internal controls; and view of possible role for supervisors.

Management oversight

Many banks noted that awareness of operational risk at the board of director or senior management level has been increasing. The focus on operational risk management as a formal discipline has been recent but was seen by some banks as a means to heighten awareness of operational risk. The greater interest in operational risk was reflected in increased budgets for operational risk measurement, monitoring and control, as well as in the assignment of responsibility for measuring and monitoring operational risk to new or existing risk management units.

Overall the interview process uncovered a strong and consistent emphasis on the importance of management oversight and business line accountability for operational risk. Senior management commitment was deemed to be critical for successful corporate risk management. Banks reported that high-level oversight of operational risk is performed by boards of directors, management committees or audit committees. In addition, most respondents referred to the important role of an internal monitor or ' watchdog', such as a risk manager or risk committee, product review committee, or internal audit, and some banks identified several different internal watchdogs, who were all seen as important, such as the financial controller, the chief information officer and internal auditors. The assignment of formal responsibilities for operational risk measurement and monitoring is far from universal, with only about half of the banks interviewed having such a manager in place.

Virtually all banks agreed that the primary responsibility for management of operational risk is the business unit or, in some banks, product management. Under this view, business area managers are expected to ensure that appropriate operational risk control systems are in place. Many banks reinforce this risk attribution and responsibility through charging operational losses to the related business or product area. In an earlier survey of internal audit issues, some supervisors noted the trend to conduct more internal control reviews in the business line, rather than in independent units such as internal audit. Several respondents to the operational risk survey noted the creation of new controls or risk management in business lines to assist in the identification and control of risk.

Several banks noted one potential benefit of formalizing an approach to operational risk. That is the possibility of developing incentives for business managers to adopt sound risk management practices through capital allocation charges, performance reviews or other mechanisms. Many banks are working toward some form of capital allocation as a business cost in order to create a risk pricing methodology as well.

Risk measurement, monitoring and management information systems

Definition of operational risk

At present, there is no agreed upon universal definition of operational risk. Many banks have defined operational risk as any risk not categorized as market or credit risk and some have defined it as the risk of loss arising from various types of human or technical error. Many respondent banks associate operational risk with settlement or payments risk and business interruption, administrative and legal risks. Several types of events (settlement, collateral and netting risks) are seen by some banks as not necessarily classifiable as operational risk and may contain elements of more than one risk. All banks see some form of link between credit, market and operational risk. In particular, an operational problem with a business transaction (for example, a settlement fail) could create market or credit risk. While most banks view technology risk as a type of operational risk, some banks view it as a separate risk category with its own discrete risk factors.

The majority of banks associate operational risk with all business lines, including infrastructure, although the mix of risks and their relative magnitude may vary considerably across businesses. Six respondent banks have targeted operational risk as most important in business lines with high volume, high turnover (transactions/time), high degree of structural change, and/or complex support systems. Operational risk is seen to have a high potential impact in business lines with those characteristics, especially if the businesses also have low margins, as occurs in certain transaction processing and payments-system related activities. Operational risk in trading activities was seen by several banks as high. A few banks stressed that operational risk was not limited to traditional 'back office' activities, but encompassed the front office and virtually any aspect of the business process in banks.

Measurement

Most banks that are considering measuring operational risk are at a very early stage, with only a few having formal measurement systems and several others actively considering how to measure operational risk. The existing methodologies are relatively simple and experimental, although a few banks seem to have made considerable progress in developing more advanced techniques for allocating capital with regard to operational risk.

The experimental quality of existing operational risk measures reflects several issues. The risk factors usually identified by banks are typically measures of internal performance, such as internal audit ratings, volume, turnover, error rates and income volatility, rather than external factors such as market price movements or a change in a borrower's condition. Uncertainty about which factors are important arises from the absence of a direct relationship between the risk factors usually identified and the size and frequency of losses. This contrasts to market risk, where changes in prices have an easily computed impact on the value of the bank's trading portfolio, and perhaps to credit risk, where changes in the borrower's credit quality are often associated with changes in the interest rate spread of the borrower's obligations over a risk-free rate. To date, there is little research correlating those operational risk factors to experience with operational losses.

Capturing operational loss experience also raises measurement questions. A few banks noted that the costs of investigating and correcting the problems underlying a loss event were significant, and in many cases, exceeded the direct costs of the operational losses. Several banks talked in terms of possibly two broad categories of operational losses. Frequent, smaller operational losses such as those caused by occasional human errors are seen as common in many businesses. Major operational risk losses were seen to have low probabilities, but an impact that could be very large, and perhaps exceed those of market or credit risks. Banks varied widely in their willingness to discuss their operational loss experience, and only a handful acknowledged the larger losses.

Measuring operational risk requires both estimating the probability of an operational loss event and the potential size of the loss. Most approaches described in the interviews rely to some extent on risk factors that provide some indication of the likelihood of an operational loss event occurring. The risk factors are generally quantitative but may be qualitative and subjective assessments translated into grades (such as an audit assessment). The set of factors often used includes variables that measure risk in each business unit, for instance grades from qualitative assessments such as internal audit ratings, generic operational data such as volume, turnover and complexity, and data on quality of operations such as error rate or measures of business riskiness such as revenue volatility. Banks incorporating risk factors into their measurement approach can use them to identify businesses with higher operational risk.

Ideally, the risk factors could be related to historical loss experience to come up with a comprehensive measurement methodology. A few banks have started collecting data on their historical loss experience. Since few firms experience many large operational losses in any case, estimating a historical loss distribution requires data from many firms, especially if the low-probability, large-cost events are to be captured. Another issue that arises is whether data from several banks or firms come from the same distribution. Some banks interviewed had created a proprietary database of external loss experiences and other banks interviewed expressed interest in access to such data. Banks may choose different analytical or judgmental techniques to arrive at an overall operational risk level for the firm. Banks appear to be taking interest in how some insurance risks are measured as possible models for operational risk measures.

Risk monitoring

More banks have some form of monitoring system for operational risk than have formal operational risk measures. Many banks interviewed monitor operational performance measures such as volume, turnover, settlement fails, delays and errors. Several banks monitor operational losses directly, with an analysis of each occurrence and a description of the nature and causes of the loss provided to senior managers or the board of directors.

Many banks interviewed are in the process of reviewing their current risk methodologies to accommodate improved measurement and reporting of operational risk and the development of an on-line monitoring system. The time lines for such efforts vary widely, with some banks currently implementing segments of new systems and other banks still in the planning stages. A significant number of other banks interviewed are not contemplating changes to their management information systems because the bank believes its current methodology serves it well. One bank has recently implemented a new risk policy framework but stated that it was too soon to assess its effectiveness. Contrary to most respondents, one bank stated that it was satisfied with its current information systems for capturing and reporting operational risk.

Control of operational risk

A variety of techniques are used to control or mitigate operational risk. As discussed below, internal controls and the internal audit process are seen by virtually all banks as the primary means to control operational risk.

Banks touched on a variety of other possibilities. A few banks have established some form of operational risk limits, usually based on their measures of operational risk, or other exception reporting mechanisms to highlight potential problems. Some banks mentioned the importance of contingent processing capabilities as a means to mitigate operational risk.

Some banks surveyed cited insurance as an important mitigator for some forms of operational risk. Several banks have established a provision for operational losses similar to traditional loan loss reserves now routinely maintained. Several banks are also exploring the use of reinsurance, in some cases from captive subsidiaries, to cover operational losses. One bank noted that the insurer would have to quantify the amount of risk in the policy and that could provide an approach to measuring operational risk.

Policies and procedures

Several banks noted that they were devoting substantial time to reviewing, revamping and developing new policies and procedures. A few banks appear to have the goal of developing a common architecture or framework to harmonize policies and procedures across businesses and make them more user-friendly. These policies and procedures may be based on common elements across business lines or across risks.

One process that received special mention was a formal new product review process involving business, risk management and internal control functions. Several banks noted the necessity of updating risk evaluation and assessments of the quality of controls as products and activities change and as deficiencies are discovered.

Internal controls

A positive result of more interest in operational risk has been a reinforcing of the value of internal controls and fresh potential for analysing the role of internal controls in reducing or mitigating risks. Most banks noted in the interviews that internal controls are seen as the major tool for managing operational risk. The controls cited include the full range of control activities described in the Basle Committee's paper on internal controls such as segregation of duties, clear management reporting lines and adequate operating procedures. Many banks expect most operational risk events to be associated with internal control weaknesses or lack of compliance with existing internal control procedures.

Interest in formalizing an operational risk discipline appears to be coinciding with another development detected in the earlier survey of audit issues. Over the past several years, many banks have adopted some form of self-assessment programme. Much of the data for monitoring operational risk, both currently and prospectively, is generated by the responsible business unit's techniques for self-assessment of its internal control environment. The results of such self-assessments can be among the factors used to evaluate operational risk, along with internal audit ratings and external audit or supervisory reviews. At least two banks described their efforts to further enhance the incentive to discover and report problems internally by penalizing the discovery of problems by supervisors or internal audit more heavily than problems uncovered in the self-assessment process.

The activities of internal auditors were also seen as an important element of operational risk management. In particular, the identification of potential problems, the independent validation of business management's self-assessments and the tracking of problem situations with the progress toward resolving the problems were cited by several banks as important to managing operational risk. In addition to internal audit, important roles were ascribed to independent financial and internal control functions (including the audit committee). These may either be corporate-wide functions or units housed in individual business or product areas. These areas typically do not focus solely on operational risk. Moreover, some banks referred to additional resources such as external auditors and the various regulatory authorities as important stimuli in creating organizational risk controls.

View of possible role for supervisors

The comments on the possible role of bank supervisors reflected the relatively early stage of the development of operational risk measurement and monitoring. Most banks agreed that the process is not sufficiently developed for the bank supervisors to mandate guidelines specifying particular measurement methodologies or quantitative limits on risk. Preference was expressed, at this stage, for supervisors to focus on qualitative improvement in operational risk management. In this regard, many banks noted the potential for supervisors to raise the level of awareness of operational risk. The banks were more split on whether the supervisors should provide a forum to facilitate the identification of 'best practices', with some expressing reservations about the usefulness of best practices given the perceived institution-specific nature of operational risk.

The Basle Committee believes that publishing this summary of the results of its survey will provide banks with an insight into the management of operational risk. The committee will continue to monitor developments in this area. Banks are encouraged to share with their supervisors new techniques for identifying, measuring, managing and controlling operational risk.

Note

1 'Operational Risk Management', Basle Committee on Banking Supervision, September 1998, Basle.

Bibliography

Alepa, Stephen, Operational Risk Management in the Investment Industry, *Investment Management Perspective*, Coopers & Lybrand's National Investment Management Industry Group, vol. 1.

Amelia Financial Systems Ltd (1998) *Operational Risk, The Last of The Risk Frontiers?* Amelia Financial Systems Limited.

Bank of England (1995) Report of the Board of Banking Supervision inquiry into the circumstances of the collapse of Barings, HMSO.

Bankers Trust (1996) Next Frontier of Risk Management, *Corporate Finance Risk Management and Derivatives Hand Book*, pp. 12–14.

Binney, George and Williams, Colin, (1995) *Leaning into the Future*, Nicholas Brealey Publishing.

Board of Governors of the Federal Reserve System (1993) Examining Risk Management and Internal Controls for Trading Activities of Banking Organisations, SR 93-69 (FIS).

Board of Governors of the Federal Reserve System (1995) Rating the Adequacy of Risk Management Processes and Internal Controls, SR 95-51 (SUP), USA.

British Bankers Association and Coopers & Lybrand (1997) *Operational Risk Management Survey*, May.

Britt, Phil (1998) Chicago Traders Tap into Cash Markets, *Futures Industry*, Futures Industry Association, October, pp. 37–39.

Burghardt, G. (1997) World Volumes: A Mixed Bag. *Futures Industry*, Futures Industry Association, February, pp. 9–13.

Callahan, Charles V. and Nemec, Joseph (1999) Creating Value, *Journal of Strategy and Business*, http://www.strategy-business.com/technology/99108/

Carnell, Colin (1995) *Managing Change in Organisations*, Prentice Hall International.

Carr, D.G. (1996) Treasury Risk Management – Derivatives for Directors, *Treasury Risk Management Practice*, KPMG.

Chance, Don, *Brief History of Derivatives*, vol. 1, no. 34, November 1995, pp. 13–20.

Champy, James (1995) *Reengineering Management*, HarperBusiness.

Classic Financial Scandals, BCCI, Barings, Daiwa, Sumitomo, Credit Lyonnais, Bre-X etc., http://www.ex.ac.uk/~RDavies/arian/scandals/classic.html

Coopers & Lybrand (1997) Generally Accepted Risk Principles, Coopers & Lybrand.

Culp, Christopher L. and Mackay, Robert J. (1994) *Regulating Derivatives: The Current System and Proposed Changes, Regulation*, vol. 17, no. 4, http://www.cato.org/pubs/regulation

De Arie, Geus (1988) The Learning Organisation, *Harvard Business Review*, April.

Donahoe, T. (1996) Derivatives Risk Control, *Contingency Analysis*, http://www.contingencyanalysis.com/reseach/

Drucker, Peter (1988) The Coming of the New Organisation, *Harvard Business Review*, January/February.

Financial Times (1998) Derivatives soar as companies seek means of controlling risks, *Financial Times*, 30 Sept.

Financial Times (1998) Turbulence threatens flourishing markets: Open outcry is being edged out in the battle for survival as evolution points to an electronic future, *Financial Times*, Derivatives survey, 17 July.

Frost, Chris, The Resilient Organisation, *PriceWaterhouseCoopers Global Risk Management*, http://www.pwcglobal.com/extweb/NewCoLth.nsf/DocID/

Frost, C. and Chrispin, J. (1997) Risk by any other name, *Clearing and Settlement Operations and Technology Supplement*, *Futures and Options World*, pp. 18–19.

Futures and OTC World (1998) Seat Prices, *Futures and OTC World*, November, p. 73.

Gantress, Louise T. (1994) Who's Afraid of Derivatives? *STERNbusiness*, http://equity.stern.nyu.edu/Webzine/Sternbusiness/Fall94/Der.html

Gibson, Rajna, and Zimmermann, Heinz, (1995) The Benefits and Risks of Derivative Instruments: An Economic Perspective, Université de Lausanne and Hochschule St. Gallen Switzerland, http://alpha.wat.ch/genevapapers

Global Derivatives Study Group (1993) *Derivatives: Practices and Principles*, Group of Thirty, Washington DC, USA.

Hammer, Michael and Champy, James (1993) *Reengineering the Corporation*, HarperCollins, New York.

Handy, Charles (1990) *The Age of Unreason*, Hutchinson.

Handy, Charles (1993) *Gods of Management*, Arrow Business Books.

Handy, Charles (1994) *The Empty Raincoat*, Arrow Business Books.

Hull, John (1993) *Options, Futures and other Derivatives Securities*, Prentice Hall.

Irish Times on the Web (1997) Financial regulators to descend on NatWest, March 3.

Kao, John (1996) *Jamming*, HaperBusiness.

Keen, P. (1996) Electronic Commerce: How fast, How Soon? Keen Innovations, http://www.peterkeen.com/emgec1.htm

Kharouf, Jim, (1996) The copper trader who fell from grace, http://www.futuresmag.com/library/august96/intrends.html

Kim, Ted (1998) Force Majeure, *Futures and OTC World*, November, p. 25.

Kloman, H.H. (1992) *Rethinking Risk Management*, Geneva Papers, July.

J.P. Morgan & Arthur Anderson (1997) *Corporate Risk Management*, Risk Publications.

Jarrillo, J.C. (1988) On strategic Networks, *Strategic Management Journal*, Vol. 9.

Johnson, Gerry and Scholes, Kevan (1997) *Exploring Corporate Strategy*, Prentice Hall.

Jorion, Philippe (1998) *Orange County Case: Using Value at Risk to Control Financial Risk*, http://www.gsm.uci.edu/~jorion/oc/case.html

Leander, Ellen (1998) Heated Exchanges, *Treasury and Risk Management*, January/February http://www.cfonet.com/html/

LIFFE Quarterly Review (1998) *LIFFE's Strategic Review*, London International Financial Futures Exchange, March.

London International Financial Futures Exchange (1996) *Managing Risk – The Structure and Operation of Liffe*.

Lovell, M. and Gittleson, D. (1997) Smooth Operations, *The Clearing Business – Futures and Options World Supplement*, pp. 14–17.

Magnus, Arthur (1996) Management of Operational Risks in Foreign Exchange, The New York Foreign Exchange Committee, http://www.ny.frb.org

Manguire, F. (1998/9) Electronic Exchanges Face Operational Growing Pains, *Futures Industry*, Futures Industry Association, December/January, pp. 23–24.

Monroe, Allen (1998) *The Evolving Role of Chief Risk Officer*, RiskInfo, http://riskinfo.com/seminars/IQPC_Oct30_98_1/index.htm

Parikh, S. (1995) *Electronic futures markets versus floor trading: Implications for interface design*. Paper as CHI '95, Conference on Human Factors in Computing Systems, May 1995, Denver, Colorado.

Parlby, D., Knowledge Management Research Report 1998, KPMG Consulting, http://www.kpmg.co.uk/

Pascale, Richard (1991) *Managing on the Edge*, Penguin Books.

Prest, Michael (1998) Clearing and settlement: Clerks step into limelight, *Financial Times*, Derivatives survey, 17 July.

PriceWaterhouseCoopers (1998) Risk Management – Middle Market Barometer, Summer http://www.pwcglobal.com/uk/eng/ins-sol/survey-rep/bb9/bb9home_alliallsukeng.html

Regan, James (1995) *Crunch Time – How to Reengineer Your Organisation*, Century Business.

Richards, Katie K. (1996) Using Derivatives, http://www.img.logica.com/views/derivatives.html

Risk management reports, various, http://www.riskinfo.com/rmr.htm

Risk Management Reports (1996) *Risk Management: Coming of Age*, March, vol. 23, no. 3, http://www.riskinfo.com/rmr.htm

Risk Management Reports (1996) *Strategic Risk Management*, December, vol. 23, no. 12, http://riskinfo.com/rmr/rmrdec96.htm

Ross, D.A. (1994) *Risk Management and Control of Derivatives*, Deloitte Touche Ross.

Russo, Thomas (1998) Comment and Analysis: Rationalising risk – Laws cannot keep pace with rapid changes in the financial system. What we need instead is a set of core principles, *Financial Times*, 21 July.

Sakar, A. and Tozzi, M. (1998) Electronic Trading of Futures Exchanges, *Current Issues in Economics and Finance*, Federal Reserve Bank of New York, vol. 1, no. 21, January, pp. 1–6.

Sanford, C.S. and Borge, D. (1995) *Risk Management Revolution*, Bankers Trust New York Corporation, http://www.bankerstrust.com/corpcomm/speech/risk/index.html

Singapore Finance Ministry's Report (1995) The collapse in February of Britain's 233-year-old Barings Investment Bank, October.

Smithson, C., Smith, C. and Wilford, D.S. (1995) *Managing Financial Risk*, Burr Ridge, Illinois, Irwin.

Solman, Paul (1998) Risk management systems: How to find a firm base for trading, *Financial Times*, Derivatives survey, 17 July.

Stewart, T.H. (1989) *Trading in Futures*, Woodhead Faulkner.

Stulz, R. (1996) Rethinking Risk Management, *Journal of Applied Corporate Finance*, Stern, Stewart & Co, vol. 9, no. 3.

Sunday Business Post (1998) Lessons aplenty in LTCM collapse, *The Sunday Business Post, On Line*, 4 October, http://www.sbposr.ie/newspaper/041098/news/lessons.html

Tait, Nikki, (1998) Regulation: Changes create new risks, *Financial Times,* Derivatives survey, 17 July.

Tomasko, Robert (1993) *Rethinking the Corporation*, American Management Association.

Varnholr, B. Six Recent Reports on Financial Derivatives: A Critical Appraisal, http://www.finance.wat.ch/GenevaParers/paper2.htm

Venture Forward (1998) Knowledge Management: An Industry Perspective, *Backweb Technologies*, http://www.backweb.com/km/pwhpaper.html#intro

Wahler, T.L. (1998) Plugging In The Pit, *Futures Industry*, Futures Industry Association, January pp. 11–13.

Watrasiewicz, R, Consolidated Risk Management belongs to the Middle Office, TCA Consulting, http://www.tcaconsulting.co.uk/vision 13/risk.htm

Whiteley, Richard, *The Customer Driven Company: Moving from Talk to Action*, Business Books, London.

Index

A.C. Grant

Chestnut House
The Street
Little Totham, Nr Maldon
Essex   CM9 8JQ